104 Ways to ENERGIZE Your Days

Ron Ball

104 Ways to Energize Your Days
by Ron Ball

Copyright ©2017 Ron Ball
All Rights Reserved

No part of this book may be used or reproduced in any manner whatsoever without the written permission of the publisher.

ISBN: 978-1-942991-75-5

Published by:

Editorial Renuevo
www.EditorialRenuevo.com
info@EditorialRenuevo.com

Table of Contents

Introduction		9
1.	The Wharton Formula	11
2.	The Possibility Window	13
3.	Listen To Your Body	15
4.	Schmoozing	17
5.	Smell	19
6.	Get Moving	21
7.	The Relater	23
8.	Calm Down	25
9.	Grace Under Pressure	27
10.	Quick Response	29
11.	Location, Location, Location	31
12.	A Good Breakfast	33
13.	Sleep Well	35
14.	Overcoming Alligators	37
15.	LOL	39
16.	Gratitude	41
17.	Hurry Sickness	43
18.	Speed	45
19.	Contagion	47
20.	Volcano	49
21.	Generosity	51
22.	People Power	53
23.	Deep and Wide	55
24.	Core Belief	57

25.	Winning The Race	59
26.	Party Time	61
27.	Look For the Unexpected	63
28.	Rev It Up	65
29.	Youthful Vitality	67
30.	Fitness	69
31.	It's Not That Bad!	71
32.	Choose to Win	73
33.	Ha Ha Ha	75
34.	Curiosity	77
35.	What's in a Name	79
36.	Ideas	81
37.	Escape	83
38.	A Worthy Goal	85
39.	The Right Gift	87
40.	Thanks for the Memories	89
41.	A Chocolate Dream	91
42.	Look Within	93
43.	Sit Up Straight	95
44.	A Humble Heart	97
45.	Snow Days	99
46.	Courage	101
47.	Reading	103
48.	An Environment of Harmony	105
49.	Waiting for Results	107
50.	Giggles	109
51.	Zest	111

52.	Sensory Experience	113
53.	Ear Power	115
54.	Open to the Unexpected	117
55.	Posture	119
56.	Stand Up	121
57.	Get Over It	123
58.	Be Patient	125
59.	Tough Enough	127
60.	Avoid the Poison	129
61.	Invention	131
62.	The Phone Call	133
63.	Look at the Facts	135
64.	Keep Trying	137
65.	Maximum Ingenuity	139
66.	Think First	141
67.	Be Aggressive	143
68.	Needless Enemies	145
69.	Don't Stop Believing	147
70.	The Generosity Surprise	149
71.	The Challenge of Change	151
72.	Improvement	153
73.	Expect a Miracle	155
74.	It's Not Over Yet	157
75.	Flex	159
76.	Yawn	161
77.	Be Careful What You Say	163
78.	Do What It Takes	165

79.	The No Complaint Zone	167
80.	Read the Signals	169
81.	Sleep Well	171
82.	Mental Clarity	173
83.	Move Up	175
84.	Order	177
85.	Embrace the Unexpected	179
86.	What You Have in Common with Slime Mold	181
87.	Out of the Box	183
88.	It's Never Too Late	185
89.	The Ultimate Sacrifice	187
90.	Staying Young	189
91.	Prepare for the Unexpected	191
92.	Loyalty	193
93.	Act Young	195
94.	Keep Going	197
95.	Unique	199
96.	Celebrate Yourself	201
97.	Resilience	203
98.	The Happiness Genius	205
99.	Make Your Fears Flee	207
100.	An Early Start	209
101.	BIG	211
102.	It's Not About You	213
103.	How To Win	215
104.	Strike Quick	217

Introduction

Welcome to the exciting world of daily inspiration.

Just as it is important to have breakfast every morning so your body is pumped with essential nutrients, so too you need to feed your soul with emotional and spiritual nutrition. Your health and energy depend on a regular diet of the right vitamins and minerals, and your inner health and energy depend on dynamic, positive input.

Every morning, I read the Bible and a section from the classic devotional book, *My Utmost for His Highest* by Oswald Chambers. Sometimes I add a motivational book that inspires me to improve my life and my success. This morning feast fires me up for the day and gives me encouragement and focus. This content is like rocket fuel that launches me into greater happiness and achievement—which is why I am so eager to introduce you to the fun and powerful stories in this book. Each segment starts with an unusual story followed by a positive lesson for your day. It concludes with a verse from the Bible that locks in the message. Each reading is simple and easy to understand. The lessons are happy ways to have a better life for you and your family.

These regular "energy sandwiches" were created when my son Jonathan walked into our kitchen one day in 2012 with an idea. He explained that he had noticed tremendous response from thousands of people who listened to me in seminars around the world. He recognized that much of the positive reactions were based on the stories and uplifting lessons I researched and taught at the events. Jonathan suggested that I write a weekly inspirational message to send to people on our mailing list and to post on our two Facebook pages. He even had a fun name, "Ballpoints."

I agreed and began to research and write "Ballpoints." Immediately, people began to message us that the week's "Ballpoint" had blessed and helped them. Many of them were surprised that the insights were so interesting and important.

I have continued to follow through on my son's idea, and the results have been spectacular. Now thousands of people receive and read the "Ballpoints" every week. God has blessed this outreach.

This book contains 104 "Ballpoints" selected from the hundreds written. There are enough so you can read two every week for a year. I suggest Monday (to start your week) and Wednesday (to encourage you to keep going), but you can do any schedule you want. Twice a week, feed yourself with the spiritual and emotional nutrition of "Ballpoints." Enjoy these "happy meals."

Share this book with friends and family who might need an extra boost every week. Have your children or grandchildren read them; they are not complicated. Spread the joy.

Remember that you can read each week's "Ballpoint" on our Facebook pages or send your email to ChooseGreatness.com.

God bless you, and God bless your success. I pray these thoughts will elevate you to greatness every week.

1 - The Wharton Formula

Edith Wharton was born in 1862 to an American family. She had all the advantages of wealth, education, and social connections. She published her first work (a volume of poems) when she was 16 and her first non-fiction book, on the decoration of houses, fourteen years later at the age of 30. She published her first novel at 40.

Following the novel, she won multiple awards, including the French Legion of Honor and the American Pulitzer Prize. She eventually became one of the most famous and widely read authors in the world. Many of her books, such as *The Age of Innocence*, have been adapted into films, to wide acclaim.

In 1934, at the age of 72, she published a memoir, *A Backward Glance: An Autobiography*. In that final work, she gave her formula for a full and happy life. She wrote, "One can remain alive long past the usual date of disintegration if one is unafraid of change, insatiable in intellectual curiosity, interested in big things, and happy in small ways."

Let me separate her words into what I call **The Wharton Formula**. She highlights four keys to what she calls the way to "remain alive":

1. Unafraid of change. Change is common. It is smart to make friends with change and use it to improve your life. Always look ahead and prepare for what might happen. Be as ready as you can for different possibilities. See change as an opportunity for incredible adventure. It can launch you in wonderful new directions that can energize your life.
2. Insatiable intellectual curiosity. This keeps your brain young. When Dr. David Snowden of the University of Kentucky studied the Roman Catholic nuns of Mankato, Minnesota, he

found that, even in their eighties and nineties, they had the fresh, young minds of thirty-year-old women. He observed that they continually stretched their intellectual boundaries. They worked crossword puzzles and learned Russian (in their eighties!) so they could read nineteenth century Russian literature.
3. Interested in the big things. Focus on the big things in life. Dream great dreams that are worthy of your life. Think about God and His purpose for you; center your thoughts on love, family, and friendship. Don't waste your time on petty distractions. You can measure yourself by what it takes to upset you.
4. Happy in small ways. Learn the art of simple pleasures. Yesterday evening, I read a book with my wife, Amy, in front of a blazing fire. It was fantastic. This morning, I walked for three miles along a quiet, tree-lined street and enjoyed the exercise and fresh air of a clear, sunny morning. It was great. Simple pleasures can satisfy your soul.

I like the Wharton formula. It makes sense to me. I hope you like it as well. Remember,

"Blessed is the one who finds wisdom, and the one who gets understanding." (Proverbs 3:13 ESV)

2 - The Possibility Window

I was in the bathtub when it happened. Amy and I had volunteered to help for two weeks with a Christian drug program in Pittsburgh, Pennsylvania. We were both speaking to groups of teenagers every day in an effort to guide them off drugs and into a positive commitment to Christ. The work was difficult and demanding.

We were staying at the program director's home, a stunning Victorian house in a suburb of the city. One afternoon, I decided to soak in a hot bath. As I drowsed in the water, I began to review the week and pray for God to give me ideas to improve the program. I was tired and discouraged. I suddenly remembered that Amy had asked me to read a new author she had discovered, Dr. Robert Schuller. He had written a series of books on what he called "possibility thinking." I reached toward a chair, retrieved the book, and began to read. For the next hour, my mind exploded with possibilities; I was flooded with inspiration. The information was so energizing that I did not even notice when the water grew cold. I read until I finished. I could not restrain my excitement. I came out of the bath, dried off, wrapped myself in a towel, and hurried into the bedroom. I woke Amy from a nap and told her God had answered my prayer for inspiration. I was on fire with positive thinking.

That night, I was a different speaker. I walked down in front of my restless teenage audience and began to tell them of the amazing possibilities built into each of them. As I told them the incredible things God could do in them, they began to wake up to their possibilities. That night, our program went nuclear; the response was tremendous. There are men and women today who have lived changed lives because of that week.

Amy and I heard that Schuller was speaking in Ft. Lauderdale,

Florida. We used the last of our money, drove to Florida, and heard Schuller live. We were electrified. My mind was spinning with possibilities. We began to read as many positive books as possible. (The one that impacted me the most was *The Magic of Thinking Big* by David J. Schwartz.) The more we expect big things, the more God blesses us. Amy and I learned that positive expectations have power to move lives.

I want you to put on your "possibility" glasses today. Open your possibility windows; learn to see the good in every situation. When you do this, you will see a new world. When I focused on the difficulties and problems of the teenagers in the drug program, I became discouraged. When I started to look for the possibilities, everything changed.

Let me suggest the following:

1. Examine your most pressing challenge. Identify at least one possibility that is hidden in the challenge.
2. Review your immediate relationships. Can you see positive possibilities that you can develop?
3. Discover the possibilities that exist just because of where you live.
4. Make a list of five possibilities that are available to you because of your unique personality and background.

You may be sitting on a gold mine of amazing possibilities— you just need to see them. Sometimes you need to dig in your own backyard and see what's there. Your treasure may be where you already are.

The Bible says, *"He has made everything beautiful in it's time."* (Ecclesiastes 3:11 ESV)

The possibilities are endless!

3 - Listen to Your Body

I recently ordered a cheeseburger at a restaurant. I had enjoyed a cheeseburger before at the same establishment and remembered its exceptional flavor. When the sandwich arrived, it looked as delicious as I recalled. It was hot, juicy, and piled high with fresh tomatoes. I smiled in anticipation, opened my mouth, and took an excited bite. Instantly something went wrong. The flavor was strange and offensive; a sour sensation assaulted my taste buds. I couldn't take another bite; I knew it would be a mistake to continue.

The human body gives unmistakable signals when something is wrong with food. It also sends signs in other areas as well: When you need sleep, you become sleepy. When you are thirsty, you seek water. When you are hungry, you eat. It is always smart to listen to your body.

In 1932, Professor Walter Cannon wrote a book that has since become a classic in human physiology titled *The Wisdom of the Body*. In this work, Professor Cannon introduced and popularized the concept of "homeostasis," which health writer Gretchen Reynolds calls, "the desire of the body to keep itself in balance and steady in its operations." Cannon, in commenting on homeostasis, wrote that "somehow the unstable stuff of which we are composed has learned the trick of maintaining stability."

Reynolds also says (in reference to sensitivity to your body) that "there are times when you either can't keep up with your intended exercise or you know that you've been overdoing things. Muscular aches that don't go away after about three days, most exercise experts say, can indicate an incipient over-use injury. Slow down or stop exercising for the time being and consult a doctor or physical therapist." Dr. Frank Booth, a professor of biomedical sciences at the University of Missouri, emphasizes that overuse injuries are so common because they are over-use injuries. He implies that we should know better than to push when we should rest. We should "listen to our bodies."

Learn sensitivity to your internal signals. Your body is designed to stay in balance. Pay attention to what it's telling you.

Let me suggest the following:

1. When you are tired; don't push. Rest. When God finished the creation of the world He rested—so should you.
2. If you show signs of sleep deprivation such as drowsiness, irritability or difficulty concentrating, then increase the amount of time you sleep. Don't depend on coffee or energy drinks when your body is telling you it needs sleep.
3. Eat slowly so you can allow your body to signal when your stomach is full. You will feel better and improve your health.
4. If you feel down, do something. Take a walk; visit someone you like. Depressive emotions thrive in isolation.

The Bible says in Psalm 127:2, *"In vain you rise early and stay up late, toiling for food to eat—for he [God] grants sleep to those he loves."* (NIV)

Listen to your body. God has programmed balance into your very cells.

4 - Schmoozing

What is schmoozing?

In his book, *The Golden Rule of Schmoozing: The Authentic Practice of Treating Others Well*, Aye Jaye pretty much defines it as his title suggests: "the authentic practice of treating others well." To illustrate, he writes, "One time I was flying through Chicago, a number of flights got delayed, and the airport was chaos. I was able to get myself rebooked … but I watched the airport concierge taking care of disgruntled customers. He stood there like a traffic cop getting the entire matter settled in no time at all. I was very impressed, so I had a conversation with him. We exchanged business cards. That afternoon, I wrote to the CEO of the company to tell him what a great person he had in place at O'Hare. The next time I came through the airport, the concierge met me at the gate to thank me for the nice letter and invited me to the airline lounge. As we talked, we found that we shared the hobby of boating. Since that time, we have gotten together for a number of boating trips."

Once, I was waiting to cash an out-of-state check at a bank in a town where I was speaking. There was a long line, so I passed the time by watching people. Everyone seemed nervous. I soon saw why. The woman teller was hostile and obnoxious. She was difficult with every person she helped. I watched, waited, and planned my strategy. When it was my turn, I smiled, and complimented her appearance. I told her that I noticed she was wearing an unusual pin and said it reminded me of one owned by my grandmother, whom I loved very much (all true). She smiled in return, cashed my check (without identification), and told me to come back; she would be happy to help me anytime.

Both stories demonstrate the art of schmoozing. In both situations, we were simply nice to people. In the Chicago story,

Jaye complimented the airline employee and even wrote a letter of commendation. In my story, I also complimented the woman and commented on a pin that obviously made her feel special.

Jaye asks, "Are you willing to give 5 percent more than the current tipping rate? Are you willing to listen to a joke you've heard without interrupting to say, 'I've heard that one before'"? If you answer yes, Jaye says you are ready to learn the art of schmoozing.

Let me suggest:

1. Do all the good you can. Amy and I always leave a tip in hotel rooms for maids we don't know. Why? Because the maids are usually women who have little money and work hard to help their families. We want to bless them and add some joy to their day.
2. Don't add stress to other people. Find ways to make life easier for everyone you meet.
3. Compliment people as often as you can.
4. Be patient.
5. Follow the classic Golden Rule. Do to others as you would have them do to you.
6. Make people happy. Do unexpected, fun things for waiters, sales clerks, toll booth operators and other people who enter your daily world.
7. Give and you will receive. Jesus says, *"Give, and it shall be given to you." (Luke 6:38 YLT)* When you happily schmooze people, they are much more likely to help you in return.

Have fun, do good and make someone's day. God will bless you when you bless others.

5 - Smell

Research at Harvard Medical School's Institute for Circadian Physiology indicates that the right smell can boost mental alertness. Research in Japan has found a connection between smell and behavior. The University of Cincinnati tested the effect of smell on workers and discovered that the right fragrance kept people more alert and improved their performance (especially on routine tasks). Surprising research on brain waves at Toho University in Japan identified specific scents that either caused the brain to relax or to become stimulated. Scientists even found smells that made the operation of certain parts of the brain more efficient. Researchers at the Rensselaer Polytechnic Institute in Troy, New York, claim that people who work in a pleasantly scented environment are 25 percent more productive, more efficient, have more confidence, and are better at resolving conflict.

The human nose can potentially detect over 7,500 different smells. Because smell is directly registered by the brain (the only one of the five senses that is), the right smell can actually create changes in feelings, energy levels, even memory. Dr. Lewis Thomas said that smell "contain[ed] all the great mysteries." Harold Bloomfield, MD, writes, "Every breath you take passes currents of air molecules over the olfactory sites in your nose and odors flood the nerve receptors in your nasal cavities, where five million cells fire impulses directly to the brain's cerebral cortex and limbic system—the mysterious, ancient, intensely emotional area of the brain where you experience feelings, desires and wellsprings of creative energy. Certain scents seem to activate specific chemical messengers, or neurotransmitters, in the brain."

Research has found that certain scents do certain things: The scents of peppermint and lemon seem to quickly boost energy. Lavender seems to help with relaxation. The scents of honeybuns and vanilla seem to encourage personal and sexual closeness.

Let me suggest the following:

1. Monitor yourself for one week. Record in a notebook how you feel when you encounter particular smells.
2. Go to both a candle shop and a fragrance store and sample different scents. Note how you feel with each experience.
3. Place the fragrances that make you feel the happiest in key locations in your home and/or office. My wife Amy places fragrant candles in each room of our home. It's great!
4. Check the fragrances you wear and see how they make you feel. Ask family and friends how they feel when they smell those fragrances.

The Bible says that you are *"fearfully and wonderfully made [by God]."* (Psalms 139:14 NIV) He has given you so many ways to enjoy life; smell must be one of them.

Make your life smell better and your life can be better.

6 - Get Moving

Many of you know that I have been a dedicated runner for over twenty years. I started running on July 2, 1992, while speaking at a meeting in Reston, Virginia, and I have never stopped. I run in every location, in all types of weather, and clock between 25 and 30 miles a week. I sleep well, I have a quick, clear mind, and I digest food easily. I feel wonderful. I am convinced that my daily exercise contributes to all these healthy results.

I am not advising you to run, but I am encouraging you to get moving and do something physical every day. Amy doesn't run, but she does walk one or two miles with me every night. The important thing is to do something.

Recently, I discovered research that confirms the value of regular exercise. Dr. John Ratey is an Associate Clinical Professor of Psychiatry at Harvard Medical School A.J. Jacobs, in commenting on Dr. Ratey's information writes, "Exercise, argues Ratey, improves your brain in both the short term (you're sharper for the couple of hours after aerobic activity) and the long term (it staves off brain aging and Alzheimer's). It bucks up the brain in all sorts of areas, including focus, memory, mood and impulse control." Jacobs also found that in a study in the *Research Quarterly for Exercise and Sport,* "Georgia students who did forty minutes of daily exercise showed more academic improvement than those who did twenty minutes a day. Those who got no exercise showed no improvement."

Jacobs returns to Dr. Ratey and further says, "On a cellular level, Ratey says, exercise increases neuroplasticity [brain flexibility and learning], blood flow, and levels of a protein called 'brain-derived neurotrophic factor' (BDNF), which he nicknames, 'Miracle-Gro for the brain.'"

Obviously, exercise is good for your brain; and this research doesn't even mention the known benefits of exercise for your heart and muscles.

My recommendation is simple: Get out and get moving. If you have not exercised for years, check with your doctor and make a plan based on his advice. Raise your level of fitness, and you can improve your health. You might even live longer.

Do the following:

1. Start slow and simple. Try a brief walk.
2. Try to find fitness friends who will do activities with you.
3. Increase (gradually)your level of activity.
4. Make exercise fun. Have a good time!

God gave you your body; He considers it important. It is significant that when God points out young David as the next king of Israel to the prophet Samuel, He specifically comments on his health and fitness: *"He was glowing with health and had a fine appearance and handsome features." (1 Samuel 16:12 NIV)*

7 - The Relater

Max Schuster and Richard Simon were friends and partners. They decided to join forces and build a publishing company in New York City. They called the new venture Simon & Schuster. Today it has become one of the largest publishing houses in the world.

In 1928, Edward Bernays, the father of modern advertising, met a young woman at a party. Joan Lowell has been described by Melissa Katsoulis in her book as, "The talk of the town not only for her impressively robust physique, spirited personality and deep brown eyes, but for the wonderful tales she told about her life at sea … she would from time to time give lectures about her exploits on her father's trading vessel, the 'Minnie Caine', on which she spent the first seventeen years of her life as the only woman on board." Her lectures included stories of strange sea rituals, exotic island cultures, daring adventures, and even shipwreck and near-death experiences. Bernays was so impressed, he introduced Lowell to a literary agent, George Bye, who was well-known for hosting lunches where he would present new talent. At one of these events, Bye introduced Lowell to Simon and Schuster. They were so impressed with Joan they offered her a contract to publish her life story. When her book, *Cradle of the Deep*, was released in 1929, it became a huge best-seller and quickly provided Joan with over $50,000 in royalties, a substantial sum at that time.

Simon and Schuster were congratulating themselves when it was revealed that Joan was a fraud. She was actually Helen Wagner, a small-time actress from California, who had barely been to sea at all. She had lied about her past and created a false record of her experiences. The scandal and embarrassment were immense.

What enabled an unknown woman to fool the literary establishment of America? The answer was simple: She was a relater. She networked her way into the New York social scene. She became friends with Bernays, who knew everyone. He introduced her to the agent George Bye, who introduced her to the publishing giants, Max Schuster and Richard Simon. She used contacts and relationships to advance her fraudulent career.

What is your lesson in all this? The key to advancement is often who you know. You need to improve your "relater" skills. You need to learn the art of networking.

Let me suggest the following:

1. Make a list of who you know. Take your time and make as complete a list as possible. Every time you record a name, write down what that person does. Ask yourself, is this a person who can help me with my life's goals?
2. Make a list of people you want to meet. Write down why beside each name.
3. Start to contact each person on your list. Be prepared to give a reason for your contact. Meet people for lunch or coffee. Do something to relate to each person.
4. Find something you can do to help the people on your list.
5. Increase your relater skills by writing notes of appreciation and giving people words of encouragement. Get in touch with old friends.
6. Go to meetings where you can have contact with the kind of people you want to know. Much of success is just showing up.

The Bible says in Romans 12:13 to, *"practice hospitality."* (NIV) The word means to be generous in your service to and support of other people. It is a form of advanced friendliness. You should become a hospitable person who is generous in relationships.

If Joan Lowell could do what she did through a network of relationships, what you could accomplish with the same approach?

8 - Calm Down

There was no warning. I was sitting at a traffic light waiting to exit a shopping center at 9 p.m. on a Saturday night. It was a crisp spring evening, so my windows were up. I was listening to the radio. Without any warning, a man appeared at my window. I could not hear his words but saw that he was wildly gesturing and yelling.

I lowered my window and asked if he needed help. He glared a moment then cursed at me. He told me he was in the vehicle behind me and wanted to know why I had not moved. I replied that I was sitting at a red light. He said that he wanted to turn right, and I was in his way. I was going straight and not turning right. This made no difference to him. He screamed that I was a stupid ##!!**&*##@ and should get out of his way.

A short time after this, I was in an airport and overheard a businessman speaking to two airline attendants. He was overflowing with anger that his flight had been canceled. They patiently explained that a snowstorm had disrupted travel, but he continued to verbally abuse them even though it did nothing to benefit him or change his situation.

Let me encourage you to calm down and hold your temper. Bill Hybels, the senior pastor of Willow Creek Community Church near Chicago, says that he once encountered two staff members having an argument. He watched as the two became more and more riled. He stopped them and said that he was instituting a new rule: Whenever a disagreement occurred, he wanted everyone to stop, calm down, and then resume the discussion. He explained that angry words are like gasoline on a fire; they only make matters worse. In writing about this incident, he said that whenever you see a conversation getting hot, you should immediately cool it down:

1. Stop to take a moment and calm yourself. Psychological studies have found that you have three to five seconds before you explode. Train yourself to use this window to stop yourself before you say or do something you might regret.
2. Lower your voice and slow your speech. I have a very successful friend who always responds to a stressful situation by purposefully lowering his voice and making himself speak slowly. I have watched as this technique calms people and defuses potentially damaging moments. I have seen it work every time.
3. Take a step back. When you do, you physically send a calming signal. You can ease tension by this simple action.
4. Breathe slowly in and out. This will instantly begin to de-stress you.
5. Pray for God's help.

The Bible says, *"A gentle answer turns away wrath, but a harsh word stirs up anger."* (Proverbs 15:1 NIV) And *"The patient are better than warriors, and those who rule their temper, better than the conqueror of a city."* (Proverbs 16:32 NABRE)

Remember that calm keeps you in control.

9 - Grace Under Pressure

Nobel Prize-winning author Ernest Hemingway once described a real man as having "grace under pressure." David Halberstam, writing about Joe Torre (former manager of the American baseball team the New York Yankees) used the same phrase to describe him. Halberstam compared Torre's strength to what he considered to be the phony tough-guy image of George Steinbrenner, owner of the Yankees when Torre was manager.

Halberstam wrote in an article for ESPN.com on December 5, 2001, "One of the things that has always fascinated me when looking at men who are engaged in fierce pursuits, in the military or sports ... is the difference between being strong and being tough ... [acting tough causes] a certain amount of swaggering, bullying and tough guy talk. Torre is, very quietly, something different. He is quietly strong."

Recently, I was flying back from Europe to the United States and observed both grace under pressure and the lack of it several times. When we were on the runway in Frankfurt, Germany, preparing for take-off, a passenger's seat belt unsnapped. The flight attendant unsuccessfully tried to fix the belt, gave up, and announced that we would have to return to the gate. Groans filled the compartment until an elderly gentleman calmly asked for a moment, bent over the passenger with total focus, and reattached the seat belt. People applauded, and we were on our way because one man did not panic and calmly solved the problem.

On my connecting flight in Detroit, Michigan, we were preparing to leave the gate when the flight attendant announced that because a passenger had pointed out that the rubber insert of an armrest was loose, we would be delayed until a mechanic arrived. The mechanic came on board 10 minutes later, wrapped masking tape around the armrest, and left. We were relieved—

until the pilot announced that we could not leave until the mechanic filed his report. When an hour passed in the hot, stuffy aircraft, the pilot apologized and said that the paperwork had been lost, the mechanic could not be found, and the process would have to start over.

At this point, a passenger in front of me began to yell and wave his arms. He exploded with anger and began to verbally abuse the flight attendant. When he calmed down, the man next to me, a very wealthy businessman, leaned over and whispered in my ear, "Doesn't he know that his outburst accomplishes nothing? It only increases his stress and creates embarrassment." The irate passenger needed grace under pressure.

Remember:

1. When you explode, it makes you look weak.
2. You will be recognized as a leader if you stay calm. People follow those who show self-control.
3. You must stop to consider the results you want in a stressful situation. Act in a way that will help you get positive results.
4. You must also turn off the bad language and angry words. When you speak clean, positive words, you cool off the situation and help calm everyone else. While guiding the Indianapolis Colts to the Super Bowl title, Coach Tony Dungy led his team without profanity. He earned the respect of his players and the fans.
5. Use the five second rule. You have about five seconds before you lose control. Use those five seconds to cool down and affirm your own self-control.

"Patience is better than strength. Controlling your temper is better than capturing a city." (Proverbs 16:32 NCV) Stay calm and in control. People will follow you with respect.

10 - Quick Response

A recently published guide to gentlemanly behavior says that when responding to a message, a gift, or an invitation, one should always respond quickly. This is a basic principle of good relationships.

After my first meeting with Charles Stanley, a powerful pastor who is broadcast on over 250 television stations, I mailed him a check in support of his Christian ministry. I received a handwritten thank-you note three days later. When I gave George H.W. Bush a recording I had done, I received a thank-you the same week. This is a mark of class and respect.

My daughter, Allison, an elected member of the Student Bar Association in law school (also president of the Federalist Society and co-president of the Christian Legal Society), told me numerous stories of law students who would verbally promise to come to an event and then not show up. She said that the majority of personal invitations were not even acknowledged. She would send personal notes from the Bar Association and receive little response. The students could have strengthened their important networks by simply being quick to respond.

I spoke recently with the CEO of a large, growing company who understands that he is measured by the speed of his response to his clients. He told me that he answers every message within 24 hours and personally acknowledges every gift sent to his office. He does this as a demonstration of respect to the person who sent the message or the gift. He has built a web of trust that supports the success of his business.

The wealthiest man I know always thanks people for what they send. Another leader I know has his assistant research (and send a query to) all possible contacts for someone to be sure that the person received his message of appreciation. A six-term United States congressman told me that 90 percent of success is just showing up. When you quickly respond to a request, you create a positive response in return. I also have a friend in Thailand who is the best quick responder I know. He always answers with speed and consideration. I believe this is one of the reasons he is so financially successful.

Let me suggest the following:

1. Show people they matter by trying to answer every message the same day. If you are unusually busy, make sure you answer within 24 hours.
2. Commit only to that which you intend to keep. Go to every event you promise to attend. This will make you stand out as a leader and will earn you loyalty and respect.
3. Explain and apologize quickly if something unavoidable interferes with your response.
4. Tell the truth when you cannot do something. People are often planning on your attendance and will appreciate your honesty.
5. Support your friends. When they have an event, always try to go; your presence builds the friendship. Do your best to always be there for them. They will remember your support.
6. Express genuine appreciation for every gift. It may not be what you would have picked, but it is what someone sincerely wanted to give you. Make certain he knows you are grateful.

The Bible says *"Be devoted to one another in love. Honor one another above yourselves."* (Romans 12:10 NIV)

Remember that you honor people by your quick response.

11 - Location, Location, Location

I grew up in the Cumberland Mountains of southeastern Kentucky. When I was eight years old, I began hiking, either by myself or with friends. This was normal. I received clear instructions from my parents about everything from finding directions and understanding safe plants to dealing with wildlife. Even at such a young age, I was trained to be aware of my surroundings and other safety techniques. Each day after school, I (and sometimes my friends) would make for the hills. It was my favorite part of growing up. To this day, I have a deep love of hiking and climbing, of forests and mountains.

Early one Saturday morning, I asked my friend Steve to climb with me to a dramatic rock formation. We called it the Three Story Caves. My idea was to leave at dawn, hike to the caves, build a fire, cook and eat breakfast, then spend the rest of the day exploring. Everything went well until just after noon. We had decided to follow a series of ridges that we had never walked before, and we were soon completely lost. We were so sure of our skills and experience that we had made no plan. We were so certain that we would always know our location that we had not even brought a compass.

We wandered for eight hours until the sun began to set. Just before dark, we found a trail and descended over 1,000 feet to a road. Two more miles brought us to a gas station that had a phone. I called my father, who came to pick us up. We were exhausted.

The lesson here is to remember the critical importance of planning. We became lost because we had no plan, no compass, and no way to orient ourselves in the wilderness.

You need to plan your actions. You should always have a map

that gives your life location and shows you where to go. When you plan, you protect yourself; you create options.

Let me alert you to the following:

1. A plan should be simple and easy to follow.
2. A plan is for guidance, not stress. You can change it, if needed.
3. A plan is smart. It is an intelligent way to know where you're going and how to get there.
4. A plan keeps you from wasting time doing things that are not productive.
5. A plan protects you from rash, emotional reactions. It keeps you "on track".

Start with a simple plan for this week. Map out your location and plan how to reach the most important goals first. When you master a weekly goal then make one for the month, then the quarter, then the year, then multi-year blocks such as a five-year plan. You may be amazed at the freedom and success your plans can produce.

"'For I know the plans I have for you,' declares the LORD, 'plans to prosper you and not to harm you, plans to give you hope and a future.'" (Jeremiah 29:11 NIV)

Amy and I do everything with a plan. It works for us, and I believe it can work for you.

12 - A Good Breakfast

My mom makes a great breakfast. When I was growing up, Mom always provided a mammoth breakfast. We would typically have fried eggs, gravy and biscuits, fried apples, fried potatoes, fried chicken, ham, bacon, and pork chops. This extensive menu was available almost every morning. I would dream of breakfast at night and wake up with anticipation in the morning. On Saturdays, she would add pancakes. I loved breakfast. The most remarkable thing about our breakfast meals was that only three of us were there to eat. (I am an only child. Combined with my mom and dad, we made a small but happy group.) I don't eat that much now, but occasionally we still walk the five minutes to my parent's house and enjoy one of Mom's famous breakfasts.

How important is breakfast to your general health and weight control? Very important. Research has revealed that the most important result of breakfast is to speed up the process of breaking down and fully digesting your overnight food. One dietary theory is that because your metabolism slows down while you sleep, you burn fewer calories. When you eat, you fire up your metabolism. When your meal is low in fat, includes proteins (which boost the metabolism) and complex carbohydrates such as high-fiber grains, you will be more satisfied during the day and less likely to crave snacks.

Professional dietitian Kathy Stone writes, "Eating breakfast is also essential to help control eating after dinner. Surprising, but true. What you eat in the morning affects how full you feel at the end of the day. If you think that breakfast makes you hungrier, that you are actually better off on the days when you go as long as possible without eating, think again. What happens when you finally start eating? Most times you lose control." When you begin the day with the right metabolic start, your whole day can improve. You will eat more normally and more easily avoid binge eating. Dr. C. Wayne Callaway, former director of the Nutrition and Lipid Clinic at the Mayo Clinic in Rochester, Minnesota, writes that when you start the day correctly, "you will be hungry at appropriate times throughout the day and you will lose the urge to binge in the evenings."

Another reason to eat breakfast is to replenish the fuels your body needs for maximum performance. Dr. Lawrence Lamb says, "In the morning your liver will be about 75 percent depleted of glycogen [glucose-derived energy fuel]. It will already be sacrificing your body protein to manufacture glucose. If you want to protect your body protein [including muscle tissue], you had better provide some carbohydrate food early in the morning to replace the glucose. Your brain will function better too, as it needs glucose to maintain its ability to do all the complex tasks required of it."

"Then God said, 'I give you every seed-bearing plant on the face of the whole earth and every tree that has fruit with seed in it. They will be yours for food.'" (Genesis 1:29 NIV) I'm sure some of that food was for breakfast.

Have a good day!

13 - Sleep Well

How well do you sleep? Are you tired during the day? Do you have difficulty falling asleep?

If you answered yes to the last two questions, you have something in common with millions of people today. Dr. Peter Hauri, former director of the Mayo Clinic Insomnia Program writes, "Sleep is interwoven with every facet of daily life. It affects our health and well-being, our moods and behavior, our energy and emotions, our marriages and jobs, our very sanity and happiness." Dr. Harold Bloomfield writes, "There's growing evidence that the majority of adults are getting grouchier and more error-prone because we're suffering from chronic 'partial sleep deprivation' —we don't get enough sleep or, more often, we sleep poorly night after night."

Sleep research has discovered some fascinating factors that may help you sleep better:

1. Have a *time-free* bedroom. Dr, Hauri says, "Set the alarm clock if you must. But ... put the clock where it can be heard, but not seen. Then you won't wake up during the night and keep looking at the clock. People sleep better without time pressure."
2. Warm up before you calm down. According to Dr. Robert Cooper, "A brief period of moderate exercise—lasting at least 5 minutes—within 3-5 hours of bedtime, or a hot bath within 3 hours of slumber, can measurably deepen your sleep. But it's not just the exercise that's beneficial—it's the increase in body temperature. Dr. Shirley Linde writes, "If you can increase your body temperature about 3-6 hours before going to bed, the temperature will then drop most when you are ready to go to sleep. The biological "trough" deepens and sleep becomes deeper, with fewer awakenings." Dr. James A. Horne at Longborough University in Great Britain says this affect

is easily produced with a hot bath or shower within 3 hours of bedtime.
3. Free your mind from worry. Professor Robert Thayer of California State University explains the difference between the two "tiredness states". One is called "tension-tiredness", when you are tired but stressed and the other is "calm-tiredness", when you are physically tired but mentally calm. This state is most supportive of a good night's sleep. Don't examine problems or challenges before you go to bed. You can make a list of your concerns and use it as an appointment to deal with the situations later. You can also pray and give your needs to God. The Bible says, *"Do not be anxious about anything, but in everything, by prayer and petition, with thanksgiving, present your requests to God..." (Philippians 4:6 NIV)*
4. Fill your bedroom with a pleasant fragrance. Smells move into your nasal cavities where 5 million nerve receptors send messages to the cerebral cortex and limbic system. These parts of your brain then create emotional response to the smell. Research has found that two scents are especially helpful in helping to promote a restful night's sleep: vanilla almond and apple spice. If you don't want to burn a candle with these fragrances you might do potpourri instead.

The Bible says, *"In vain you rise early and stay up late, toiling for food to eat— for he [God] grants sleep to those he loves." (Psalm 127:2 NIV)*

Sleep well.

14 - Overcoming Alligators

In 1772 William Bartram was 33 years old, broke, in debt and with few prospects.

He had been born with wonderful advantages. His father was famous as the Royal Botanist for the American colonies for King George III. His family was so well-connected that Benjamin Franklin, a family friend, offered him an apprenticeship at 16. He was one of the few young men with higher education, having graduated from the College of Philadelphia. He was given enough money to buy a plantation; but he was such a poor businessman that it failed, leaving him adrift at 33—at which point everything changed.

William suddenly acted with unusual determination. He decided to follow in his father's footsteps and become a professional botanist. He had been commended by the well-known scientist Dr. John Fethergill for the quality of certain nature sketches he had done. So he contacted Dr. Fethergill and boldly asked him to finance a scientific exploration of the Florida wilderness. Fethergill said yes, and William traveled to Florida.

One experience forever changed his life. He wrote in his journal about the night he was asleep in a remote and wild area and awoke to hear a wolf stealing his food. He fervently believed that God had awakened him in time to save his life. He was shaken but decided to continue.

Another time, he found himself on the edge of a lake, watching two alligators fight to the death. When the conflict ended, he was startled to see alligators advancing toward him from all sides. He leaped into his canoe and fought them off as they repeatedly tried to drag him from the boat. One heaved itself over the side, and Bartram was only saved by ramming the barrel of his shotgun into the creature's mouth and pulling the trigger. Hundreds of alligators continued filling the water in every direction. He grounded the canoe, climbed a tree, and waited for a chance to escape. When he saw an opening, he launched the vessel and, for several days, navigated the dangerous waters. He was attacked often and used a club to beat off the animals. He finally escaped and found a safe area.

William came out of this experience a tough and courageous explorer. His fears evaporated, and he soon became famous as a botanist and researcher. His success under pressure molded him into a greater man. After battling alligators in the swamps of Florida, he never feared anything again.

What so-called alligators do you need to face and overcome? When you confront and conquer your fears, you pave the path for a greater life. The more alligators you defeat, the more confident you will become.

Joshua 1:9 says, *"Be strong and courageous. Do not be afraid; do not be discouraged, for the Lord your God will be with you wherever you go."* (NIV) This is the verse I read to my family every New Year's Eve. I am always inspired by its call to courage.

Don't ever give up. Remember, even alligators can be beaten when you never stop fighting.

15 - LOL

In 1952, MGM Studios released a happy, rollicking 103-minute film co-directed by Gene Kelly and Stanley Donen. The movie *Singin' In The Rain* was an instant hit. The film was released in the spring, and the New York Times movie review responded to the timing by saying, "Spring came with a fresh and cheerful splatter ... yesterday with the arrival of *Singin' In The Rain*.... Compounded generously of music, dance, color, spectacle, and a riotous abundance ... on the screen ... all elements of this rainbow are ... guaranteed to lift the dolors of winter and put you in a buttercup mood." One of the best scenes is when Donald O'Conner sings about laughter. As the *Times* writes, "Donald O'Conner, as Mr. Kelly's sidekick, ...has a jolly romp ... in a slapstick number entitled, *'Make 'Em Laugh!'*"

Laughter has definite health and life benefits. Dr. John Morreall writes, "The person who has a sense of humor is not just more relaxed in the face of potentially stressful situations, but is more flexible ... his imagination will ... prevent boredom and depression." Edward de Bono, MD, writes, "Humor is by far the most significant behavior of the human mind." The late Dr. William Fry Jr., who was professor emeritus of the Department of Psychology of Stanford University, said that laughing 100 times a day was a good, healthy goal. Author Norman Cousins humorously writes, "Laughter is inner jogging" because of its health benefits. Dr. Harold Bloomfield writes that, "Scientists theorize that laughter stimulates the production of brain catecholamines and endorphins, which affect hormonal levels in the body, some related to joy, an easing of pain and strengthened immune response."

Try the following:

1. Watch funny movies and read funny stories. Make sure they are

positive, uplifting and make you feel good about yourself and others. Avoid humor that demeans and insults other people.
2. Notice the humor in everyday life. My family and I enjoy watching our crazy cat and goofy dog. They are super fun to observe.
3. Laugh out loud. You will be surprised at how good you feel.

The Bible says in Proverbs 17:22, *"A cheerful heart is a good medicine." (ASV)*

Go ahead: Have a good laugh.

16 - Gratitude

Phyllis was one of the most important friends I have ever had. When she died in May 2011, our entire community reacted with grief. She had lived a full life well into her nineties and had personally influenced hundreds and indirectly touched tens of thousands. When her husband died, she had inherited a large sum of money and was committed to the support of conservative Christian ministries around the world. Her son owned a NASCAR team that won the Daytona 500 twice. She was very proud of him.

I used to visit her once a week for prayer. We would talk about the wonderful reality of Jesus Christ and bask in His amazing presence. When she prayed, we were always transferred into the miraculous. Sometimes our prayer sessions would last for hours, but I would leave refreshed and powerfully energized. God would reveal fascinating insights and show us very specific directions that worked EVERY TIME. Her friendship and spiritual guidance helped me at pivotal points in my life. She was, simply, a woman of God.

Once, at her home, I asked if she ever struggled with depression or stress. She answered by telling me how God had helped her through the unexpected loss of her husband. She described the time alone and the adjustments required. She then said something I have never forgotten. She said that during every challenge in her life, she had always maintained a grateful spirit. She would thank God in every situation. She said that when she did this, her troubles would shrink, and God's power would flow into the circumstance. She laughed and further stated that it is hard to stay down when your "attitude of gratitude" is lifting you up. She contended that in every situation, she could always find something to thank God for. What a wonderful example!

Let me suggest the following:

1. Train yourself to look for the positive in everything. You may not always be looking in the right place. Learn to see the good.
2. Replace complaining with gratitude. Become famous for a thankful spirit.
3. Ask God to reveal His purposes in your life. You may be pleasantly surprised.
4. Express gratitude and appreciation, every day to as many people as possible.

Keep positive. The Bible says in 1 Thessalonians 5:18, *"Give thanks in all circumstances." (NIV)*

17 - Hurry Sickness

The Concorde was a supersonic aircraft that flew from New York to Paris in around three and a half hours. Before its retirement from service, the Concorde fleet became an international symbol of speed and expensive travel; the passengers paid high rates to save a few hours.

Once, when a Concorde landed in New York, an electrical problem prevented the doors from opening. The Air France maintenance crew quickly arrived to handle the situation. When five minutes passed and the doors were still closed, passengers became angry and began demanding compensation from the airline. After fifteen minutes passed, the flight crew thought the passengers were on the edge of a full-scale riot and tried to create calm. All this was because of a fifteen-minute delay.

There are the same 1,440 minutes (86,400 seconds) in everyone's day. But people continually speak phrases like, "I don't have enough time"; "Time is running out"; "I am under time pressure"; and "Time is up." Some psychologists call this "hurry sickness." Some polls claim that people in Europe and the United States complain about lack of time more than a lack of money or freedom.

Health and wellness writers Dr. Harold Bloomfield and Dr. Robert Cooper write, "It's no accident that the word 'deadline' contains the word 'dead': the human body is not well-suited to time struggle. Research strongly suggests that people who suffer from 'hurry sickness' —the chronic feeling that there's never enough time—may be at increased risk for developing or aggravating health problems such as high blood pressure, heart disease, and certain forms of cancer. A 'struggle with time' is also linked to chronic anger and hostility, depression, bitterness, resentment, and sudden cardiac death (an unexpected, fatal heart attack)."

You should focus on "using your time effectively and freeing yourself from anxious watch-watching and a nagging sense of impatience, [which is] a prerequisite to success in improving your health, fitness and relationships."

In contrast, a well-ordered day can give you enough time not only to fulfill your responsibilities but also to enjoy your family and friends. You can still do activities you love, and you can still experience the pleasure of a day that is well-lived.

Here are some positive suggestions:

1. Develop what some researchers call time competence. This means organize and plan your day so that you manage time instead of feeling that you are the slave to time.
2. Learn patience. Make yourself slow down and think. Patience calms you and helps you relax.
3. Prioritize, and then stick to the priorities. The legendary entrepreneur Mary Kay Ash, who founded the multi-billion-dollar business Mary Kay Cosmetics, Inc., picked only six priorities a day and then stuck to those priorities.
4. Do not allow the priorities of other people to control you. Don't take on responsibilities because of guilt.
5. Let go and let God. You are not the ruler of the universe. You don't have to do everything, just the things that matter. God has given you enough time to do all you need to do.

The Bible says in Psalm 56:4, *"In God I trust; I will not be afraid. What can mere mortals do to me?" (CSB)*

Plan so you don't have to hurry. Experience the freedom of managing your time well for happiness and success.

18 - Speed

The cheetah is the smallest member of the family of "big cats." An adult cheetah is between 75 and 145 pounds, and males are 10 pounds heavier than females.

It is the only one of the big cats that cannot roar, although it does purr, sometimes very loudly. It has amazing eyesight and can clearly see its prey over three miles away.

The cheetah has poor night vision; therefore, it is the only big cat that hunts during the day. It is limited by its inability to climb trees. Because of its light body weight and blunt claws, it is easily vulnerable to larger predators, such as lions and leopards.

When the cheetah sights its prey, it maneuvers to within 50 feet and then springs into action. It is the fastest animal in the world; it moves from a complete stop to 45 mph in 2.5 seconds and can briefly sustain a top speed of 64 mph. The cheetah uses its superior speed to seize and subdue its victim, and then clamps its powerful jaws on the neck of the other animal. It suffocates the prey then drags it to a safe place.

One the most undervalued elements of success is speed. Napoleon revolutionized warfare by moving his armies faster than any army had ever moved. He consistently shocked his adversaries by appearing in places and positions they never expected. He used speed to conquer Europe.

You may need more speed in your own life. How long do you take to make decisions? How long do you debate your goals? How much time do you use to find and seize opportunities? One of the facts of opportunities is that they move quickly; if you don't grab them when they appear, they may not return.

Do your due diligence but then move ahead. Don't let opportunities pass. There are only so many of them.

Let me suggest:

1. When you know what you want take immediate action. Don't delay. Move!
2. When something is needed before you can go forward (such as calling someone or arranging something) do it quickly.
3. Focus on completion. Learn to be "results oriented". Never rest until you have finished what needs to be done. Don't allow yourself to do anything else until you have completed what you are doing.

The Bible says in Proverbs 18:9, *"One who is slack in his work is brother to one who destroys." (NIV)*

Nothing is ever done until you do it. Get moving!

19 - Contagion

Beverly is special. She worked for years as a skilled leader in the children's department of a large United Methodist Church in Marietta, Georgia. Whenever the kids had a bad day, the appearance of "Miss Beverly" (she was actually a Mrs., with children of her own) would instantly change the atmosphere from one of disruption to one of joy. Once, she discovered several million bees in the walls of her suburban home. She decided that since it would take time to remove the insects, she would enjoy them. She would invite guests, have them listen to the deep buzzing, and comment on how happy they sounded.

Beverly passionately loves Walt Disney World. She and her family have visited the Magic Kingdom every year for over 30 years, and she has never tired of the fun resort. My family and I were once asked by Beverly to use our motorhome to transport her clan and ours to Disney for Easter weekend. The plan to use another friend's RV collapsed when the owner got chicken pox, so Beverly called us and cheerfully asked if we would like to take everyone—her husband would pay the expenses. We agreed (it was Amy's birthday weekend, and she thought it was the ideal birthday gift). So we loaded everyone, including our six-month-old daughter Allison, and drove to Florida. It was the greatest trip we had ever experienced. I caught strep throat; but Beverly's happiness was so contagious, I still had a fantastic time.

Beverly is an example of the power of a person to emotionally influence the people around her. Your attitude is contagious, for good or bad. Dr. Robert Cooper writes about "what research psychologists call 'emotional contagion.'" That's the unconscious transmission of feelings—positive or negative—from one person to another that occurs in a flash (sometimes in a split second). You can start an epidemic of happiness when you use your "emotional contagion."

Let me suggest the following:

1. Decide to be a "happiness generator". This is what people need from you every day.
2. Choose to be a low-maintenance person. Take care of yourself. Don't continually "dump" your negative emotions on others.
3. Find something positive about every situation: I mean *every situation.*
4. Become known as the happiest person around. People will be attracted to your joy.

The Bible says, *"The joy of the Lord is your strength". (Nehemiah 8:10 NIV)*

Go ahead: Let your happiness start an epidemic!

20 - Volcano

Mount St. Helens is a popular hiking location in the American Pacific Northwest. It is 96 miles south of Seattle, Washington, and 50 miles northeast of Portland, Oregon. It attracts day hikers and campers from a radius of 200 miles. Its snow-covered summit offers satisfying views in every direction. Because of its proximity to large population centers, it always attracts large numbers of visitors. It is part of the Cascade Range, a segment of the famous Pacific Ring of Fire, which includes 160 active volcanoes. It is named after the Baron St. Helens, a friend of George Vancouver who was an 18th century explorer.

At 8:32 a.m. on May 18, 1980, Mount St. Helens blew its top in a spectacular eruption. The powerful blast killed 57 people and destroyed 250 homes, 47 bridges, 15 miles of railroad, and 185 miles of highway. Two hundred and fifty square miles of forest were completely leveled. The ash cloud that blew into the sky traveled thousands of miles and interfered with aircraft from several countries. The eruption was so violent that the mountain was reduced by over 1300 feet to its present elevation of 8,365 feet. It is the most destructive volcanic event in US history to date.

The eruption of anger in a volcano of strong negative emotions can actually harm your body as well as your relationships. Dr. Harold Bloomfield writes that "recent studies report that suppressing anger AND explosively venting it may both be linked to a death rate (from all causes) that is over two times greater than that related to 'reflective coping.' Three standard responses to anger are (1) 'anger in' -suppressing your angry feelings altogether: (2) 'anger out' -explosively venting your anger immediately; and (3) 'reflective coping' —waiting until tempers have cooled to rationally discuss the conflict with the other person or sort things out on your own…. Those people who kept their cool—who acknowledged their anger but were not openly hostile, physically or verbally-felt better faster and had superior health."

I would add that prayer and dependence on God's help can provide the power to stay calm and in control.

Let me suggest:

1. Stop before you react. You don't have to be a human volcano.
2. Take a deep breath. Count slowly to five and let your breath out. Relax your neck and shoulders. You can now respond to the situation.
3. Change your focus from winning an argument to winning over the other person. Try to understand the other individual. Revenge is not a healthy option.
4. Remember that your volcanic anger can harm the people around you (especially your family).Replace the hot lava flow with the cool breeze of kindness and thoughtfulness.
5. Ask God for help. He loves you.

The Bible says, *"In your anger do not sin': Do not let the sun go down while you are still angry, and do not give the devil a foothold."* (Ephesians 4:26–27 NIV)

Calm down. You may live longer and better.

21 - Generosity

It was July. The temperature was hot, but my finances were cold. I had just reviewed our financial picture with Amy, and the view was bleak. We had experienced an unexpected reversal due to a big real estate deal gone bad, and we were considering our options. I took a break and sat down to watch a church service by Internet. The church was one we occasionally attended, and where God had repeatedly spoken to us. We appreciated the honest, dynamic biblical leadership of the pastor and had made numerous friends. We were excited about the way the church explained a relationship with Jesus Christ. As I watched, I became aware of an inward sense of direction. At first, it seemed only a faint hint of something; but as I watched, it strengthened. After a few minutes, I knew what I was supposed to do: God was leading me to give a gift to that church. The figure of $1,000 lodged in my mind. I only had $3,000 in my bank account, with several bills due over the next three weeks. I struggled for a moment and then decided it was wiser to obey God. My good friend, Dr. Charles Stanley, had taught me that when I knew God was guiding me to do something, I should obey and leave the consequences to Him. I went to my online banking site and transferred $1,000 to the church. I felt immediate peace. When I told Amy, she (being Amy) completely agreed.

For the next three weeks, our finances became worse. We waited and continued to trust God. At the beginning of the fourth week, we had an invasion of miracles. Money poured in; speaking engagements suddenly multiplied. Our bills were paid. God gave the blessing we badly needed.

Generosity is always blessed. I encountered a Jewish hedge fund manager a few years ago. This man handles tens of billions of dollars. He lives in New York City, is politically liberal, and a professed atheist. And yet he counsels his clients to give generously (he even urges them to follow the biblical tithe principle of 10 percent). He further told me that he has observed, in the world of high finance, that those who give always receive a return. He said that he is unable to explain why this works. He even joked that the Bible must be true because this result is so consistent. A Baptist pastor friend of mine calls this "God's miraculous plan of economy." I believe it is even a proof of God's existence.

Whether you are Christian or not or even religious or not, you should try generosity. You may be surprised by the results. When you help someone else, there is a positive return to you. As another friend of mine says, "giving is the secret of living."

The Bible says in Malachi 3:10, *"'Bring the whole tithe into the storehouse, that there may be food in my house. Test me in this,' says the LORD Almighty, 'and see if I will not throw open the floodgates of heaven and pour out so much blessing that there will not be room enough to store it.'" (NIV)*

Every time we have trusted and obeyed God with our finances, He has sent us an explosion of blessing. Every time.

22 - People Power

He is 75 years old and doesn't look a day over 30. He has kept himself in terrific shape and still travels extensively. He actively supports numerous good causes and frequently volunteers to assist the United States government with special projects. His health is excellent, except for one potentially life-threatening allergy. He rarely, however, suffers a reaction because he has learned to avoid the allergen.

He is famous but tries to stay modest and humble. He is friendly and gracious and would never knowingly harm anyone. In spite of this, he has a large number of sworn enemies who just don't seem to like him. He owns a spectacular, custom-built home in the far north that has a state-of-the-art collection of amazing technology. No one is sure of his source of income, but he never seems to lack money. He lives the lifestyle of the superrich. He values his privacy so much that he spends much of his public time in disguise, and he uses an alias to keep away curious people.

He is internationally known by his designated title. He is simply the most interesting man in the solar system. You know him as Superman.

Superman was born in Action Comics # 1 in 1938. He has been the subject of books, movies, and television shows. He was also the star character in the movie Man of Steel (released in 2013) by visionary director Zack Snyder. The challenge with the Superman character was how to make a virtually indestructible and phenomenally powerful being interesting. Snyder decided that the best way to do that was to explore his needy side. In the movie, Superman struggled with the twin human (and alien) experiences of isolation and loneliness. There was a hole in Superman's heart: He needed friends and family; he needed people. He needed not to be so alone.

This is the same need we all have. You were not created by God for loneliness. You were made to interact with other people and to enjoy positive and fun relationships. You were made to fit into a social network. You need people.

Let me suggest the following:

1. Join a group that fits your interests. Play softball, do a cooking class or attend a Bible study. Get involved with a growing group, filled with interesting, growing people.
2. Reconnect with old friends. Use social media to find people from your past. Make it fun to rediscover friendships.
3. Spend true quality time with your family. Call your parents. Build up these unique relationships.
4. Volunteer to help other people. You will be blessed in return.

The Bible says in Psalm 133:1, *"How good and pleasant it is when [we] live together in unity!" (NIV)*

Make some friends.

23 - Deep and Wide

Author Dava Sobel is impressed with Jupiter. She writes in her book *The Planets*, "Jupiter more than doubles the mass of the other eight planets combined. Compared to the Earth alone, Jupiter measures 318 times Earth's mass, and 1,000 times Earth's volume."

The size of Jupiter can also be appreciated by the size of one of its most curious features, the Great Red Spot. The spot is actually a continuously churning violent wind storm. It is oval shaped and hurtles at an almost unimaginable speed around the equator. It has been observed and studied by astronomers since 1879. Since its first sighting, the storm has changed color from vivid vermilion to a pale orange. It never changes direction and always moves in the same lane, like a runaway truck on an interplanetary interstate. Whenever it encounters another storm, it sucks it in, shreds it, and simply goes on. The surface of Jupiter is a wild expanse of cyclones, lightning storms, and violent jet streams. Some storms develop and last for centuries. It seems to be a planet of, as Sobel writes, "pure weather."

But for such a dramatic planetary presence, there really is not much there. Jupiter is a gas giant with no solid surface and no physical terrain. Even if we found a way to survive the environment, there would be nothing to land on, as Jupiter is an atmosphere-only planet, lacking a solid core.

The lesson is simple: As you build your outer life, always remember to develop your inner life as well. You want to be both deep and wide. You want to have something special beneath the surface. I read recently of a major Hollywood superstar. He is one of the best-known people in the world whose movies have made billions of dollars in profits. The author of the article said the star had megawatt, world-class charisma. He also wrote that the charisma was all there was; beneath the shallow surface was no depth at all.

Make a commitment to increase what you know and improve who you are. My wife, Amy, has done this for years. She reads important books, studies her Bible, listens to helpful audios, and seeks out fascinating people; she loves personal growth. Because of this, she is a more meaningful and interesting person than when I met her, and she continues to be more so every day.

Let me suggest the following:

1. Read on a topic you know nothing about. Learn something new.
2. Google five new subjects that you have always been curious about. Stretch your knowledge.
3. Watch an informational show on television (History Channel, Discovery Channel, etc.) that you have never watched before.
4. Schedule a time every week when you think about what you have learned that week. Discuss your new insights with someone else.

The Bible says in 1 Samuel 16:7, *"For the LORD does not see as man sees; for man looks at the outward appearance, but the LORD looks at the heart."* (NKJV)

Make sure your heart is filled with something new and wonderful every day. Choose to be deep and wide.

24 - Core Belief

He grew up in obscurity, with little money and no connections.

He built a career in an industry that many people considered lightweight and shallow.

He experienced a depression so deep, after his divorce, that close friends worried for his sanity.

He attempted a major career change late in life that publicly failed.

He was routinely dismissed, by many in high positions of influence, as reckless, uninformed and limited in intelligence.

When he mounted a comeback, most people expected him to quickly fade.

He was almost 70 years old when he gambled everything on one last, daring, grasp for a dream.

His name is Ronald Wilson Reagan.

Reagan had many positive qualities, but the one most important for you today is the force of his core beliefs. He spent years developing an internal gyroscope that guided him when he flew through storms of doubt and opposition. His core kept him strong and focused. He knew what he believed about America and American opportunity, and he knew why he believed it.

Reagan believed in the exceptionalism of the American idea and the necessity for American influence. He believed in a personal God who exercises both love and judgment and is intimately involved in the affairs of men and nations. This core made him a man who could not be defeated. His core beliefs gave him the power to move a nation.

What is your core? What are you so sure of that it cannot be shaken? If you don't know, then you need to set apart time to examine your worldview and decide on your non-negotiables. What can't you live without? A solid core will ground and deepen you, so make it the foundation of your life.

Let me suggest:

1. Search your heart. Discover what matters most to you and write it in a brief, simple statement.
2. Organize your life around your core. Let your core beliefs create your cause and let your cause guide your life.
3. Research what you believe so you can effectively express your core to others.
4. Show some guts and stand for something that matters.

"Test everything. Hold on to what is good. Keep away from every kind of evil." (1 Thessalonians 5:21-22 ISV)

25 - Winning The Race

The Race Across America is a grueling competition that challenges the best cyclists in the world. Unlike the Tour de France, the American event is not a stage race. Once a cyclist starts, there is no let up. He keeps going until he either gives up or finishes. The only way to gain an advantage over other riders is to sleep less. The typical winner sleeps two hours out of every 24 and takes nine days to finish the race. The route, which travels 3,000 miles, starts in Oceanside, California, and ends in Annapolis, Maryland.

Jure Robic of Slovenia is the only five-time winner of the Race Across America. In the small world of ultra-endurance athletes, he became a legend. He was known to his friends as "Animal" and once rode 518.7 miles in 24 hours, a world record. To prepare for his races, he cycled or did workouts 6–10 hours a day. He would force himself to go without sleep for 24 hours. He would often do a 24-hour non-stop ride followed by a 12-hour break followed by another 12-hour ride. He rode 28,000 miles (more than the circumference of the earth) every year.

In the later stages of the Race Across America, his feet would swell two sizes bigger, and his thumbs would grow numb from the pressure of his hands on the handlebars. After one of his wins, his thumbs took so long to recover that he had to use two hands to turn a key.

We are all amazed at such feats of stamina. We admire the dedication and determination that drive these athletes. We envy their physical grace and power.

What drives you? What ignites your passion? What motivates you to move beyond your comfort level? What causes you to stretch for a higher place?

You need a great cause to fill your life with purpose. You need a reason to fight. You require a mission beyond yourself.

This purpose is not money. Money can pay for the purpose, but it does not work as the purpose. You need to matter. You need a connection to something bigger than yourself.

God has a unique purpose for you. You need to find it.

You need something worth giving your life for.

The Bible says in Jeremiah 29:11, *"'For I know the plans I have for you,' declares the LORD, 'plans to prosper you and not to harm you, plans to give you hope and a future.'" (NIV)*

26 - Party-Time

We were surprised by the award.

The committee visited dozens of homes in our small town. The process was secret until the final announcement. No one knew the result.

Amy had always decorated for Christmas, but this year she had been inspired. The front porch of our nearly 100-year-old home was a wonderland of Christmas dazzle. The evergreen boughs, combined with extra wide red ribbon around the porch columns, gave a festive appearance. The oversized elves and candles provided special warmth. The six-foot-tall Santa added to the magical scene. The yard was dominated by a life-size nativity area centered by a radiant Baby Jesus. A snow-covered 18th century-style lamp completed the picture.

When we were notified that we had received the community award for the most beautifully decorated Christmas house, I gave all the credit to Amy.

My wife celebrates every major holiday. She strings banners for New Year's Eve and lights fireworks into the night. She hosts a vibrant Super Bowl party (I added that one). She spreads flowers and hearts on Valentine's Day. She goes green on St. Patrick's Day. Easter is a spectacular display of crosses, lilies, eggs, and rabbits. Memorial Day is an outdoor festival of food and fun. The Fourth of July is a flag-waving extravaganza. Labor Day is a laid-back barbecue-driven family time. Halloween is filled with pumpkins and costumes. Thanksgiving is a cornucopia of harvest decorations and comfort food. Christmas is Christmas.

Every season is party time. Amy is so good at this that our family calls her the Happiness Genius.

Make your holidays special occasions for family, friends, and fantastic food. Enjoy the changes of summer, fall, winter, and spring. Celebrate life; it is God's gift.

Let me suggest:

1. Relax with your preparations. It is better to have an imperfect party than a stressful regret.
2. Focus on something special about each seasonal holiday and decorate around that theme.
3. Be simple. This doesn't have to be expensive.
4. Have fun.
5. Be more committed to other people's enjoyment than your own. The blessing you give will return to you.

The Bible says in Philippians 4:4, *"Rejoice in the Lord always. I will say it again: Rejoice!" (NIV)*

27 - Look For the Unexpected

Harry Wesley Coover, Jr. died on March 26, 2011, at his home in Kingsport, Tennessee. He was 94.

In 1951, he and a fellow chemist, Fred Joyner, were testing hundreds of compounds searching for a heat resistant substance that could be used for a coating on the outside of jet cockpits. They had already tested 909 chemical combinations when Dr. Coover decided to try the 910th. He spread the compound between the two lenses of a refractometer (instrument used to measure the speed of light rays) and found he could not separate the lenses. He momentarily went into a panic because of the loss of the expensive laboratory equipment. The machine, which cost $3000 in the1950s, was ruined.

Out of this disaster, Dr. Coover saw an opportunity. He worked on the substance for seven years, and then marketed it as a product called Eastman 910. Because of the unusual nature of the product, Dr. Coover was invited to appear on a television show called I've Got a Secret. A panel of celebrities would try to guess the occupation or invention of a guest. When the host, Garry Moore, asked the scientist to demonstrate his idea, Dr. Coover had a metal bar lowered onto the stage. He added one drop of the compound to the bar and stuck another bar to the first. He then held onto the double bar as it was lifted off the stage.

It was not until 1980 when the product was sold to the National Starch Company and given a new name that the invention became a success. The new name was Super Glue.

You should always be alert to new ideas and opportunities. You don't know what potential success is hiding in an apparently ordinary package. You should train yourself to use "expanded thinking," which means that you learn to see everything in your life as a potential for unusual development. You can maximize the commonplace into the amazing.

Try the following:

1. Take three ordinary things and imagine what you could do with them that you don't already do. (Do this every day for a week.)
2. Examine your friendships. Make a list of something your friends could contribute to your life. Is there a need they could meet?

Learn to use everything in your life wisely. The Bible says, "*Wisdom makes one wise person more powerful than ten rulers in a city.*" *(Ecclesiastes 7:19 NIV)*

28 - Rev It Up

The Jaguar changed everything.

David Davis dropped out of college and immediately tried an assortment of jobs. He sold Volkswagens and Triumphs in Ypsilanti, Michigan, worked in a men's clothing store, and filled in on a Ford assembly line. But when he saw a Jaguar XK120, he fell in love. He decided to find a way to work with cars.

He was selling advertising for *Road & Track* magazine on the west coast of the United States when he was hired by an advertising agency to write ad copy for a hot new car called the Corvette. One of the other copywriters, Elmore Leonard (who later became a best-selling novelist) encouraged him to add more "pizzazz" to his words.

In 1962, he began writing for *Car and Driver* magazine as a regular columnist (becoming editor and publisher) and later wrote for *Automotive* magazine. He once got in trouble with one of his sponsors for a review of a German luxury car when he wrote (after a test drive) that its Blaupunkt radio "could not pick up a Manhattan station from the other side of the George Washington Bridge." He eventually became an editorial director of *Motor Trend* magazine.

His columns were so popular that they were published in 1999 in a book titled, *Thus Spake David E.: The Collected Wit and Wisdom of the Most Influential Automotive Journalist of Our Time.*

He once wrote in *Car and Driver*, "I see myself as a guest in the homes of several hundred thousand car enthusiasts each month, talking about what I've driven, where I've been and who I've met. I strive to be entertaining as well as informative, because I want to be liked, to be remembered, to be invited back. It usually works." He is credited with giving *Automobile* magazine the motto, "No More Boring Cars!"

The lesson here is simple: Find your "enthusiasm" focus. Fill your life with sheer joy; fall in love with something really cool. Start an adventure; attempt something great. Make your motto: No More Boring Life!

This can be the key to attracting the right people into your life. When you are revved up, people want to be with you. Rev up others by first revving up yourself.

Get going and get happy. The Bible says in Nehemiah 8:10, that *"the joy of the LORD is your strength." (NIV)*

29 - Youthful Vitality

He made one of his biggest splashes at 91.

Sidney Harman was a true Renaissance man. His story is one of extraordinary accomplishment and youthful vitality.

When he was 35, he co-founded Harman/Kardon, a company that made and sold high-end audio equipment for residential and business use. He later developed and sold navigational devices for cars. Forbes estimated his fortune in 2010 at $500 million. He was a philanthropist who gave millions of dollars to education and the arts.

He was also an avid sportsman who played golf and tennis for most of his long life. He was a health and fitness enthusiast who jumped out of bed every morning to do calisthenics. He loved scholarship and regularly read and researched to generate new ideas. He plowed through countless books to stay on the frontiers of creative thought.

He studied physics, engineering, and social psychology. He was a knowledgeable fan of both jazz and classical music and could recite Shakespeare from memory.

In addition to his business activities, Harman was the president of a Quaker college on Long Island, New York, and he served as the United States Deputy Secretary of Commerce in the 1970s. He slowed down enough to write his memoirs, which he published at the age of 85.

He was still active in business into his nineties and, to the surprise of many, bought Newsweek magazine in August 2010, two days before his 92nd birthday. He immediately joined Newsweek to a hot young website The Daily Beast and prepared to shock the media world, even though he had no media experience.

He did everything with youthful vitality.

Let me suggest the following:

1. Pick something that makes you feel young and do it for one week.
2. Make a list of people who make you feel young and dynamic and arrange to spend time together.
3. Select a project that is exciting and doable. Make a plan to make it happen. Do the plan.
4. Ask God for a mission that will require youthful energy.

The Bible says, *"But those who hope in the LORD will renew their strength. They will soar on wings like eagles; they will run and not grow weary, they will walk and not be faint."* (Isaiah 40:31 NIV)

Let your youthful vitality flow.

30 - Fitness

He was the father of fitness.

He was, by his own admission, an emotional and physical wreck while growing up in San Francisco. He was a pimply kid who craved junk food. When he was 15 years old, he went to a lecture on diet and nutrition. For the rest of his long life, he credited this one lecture with changing everything. He began working out with weights at a time when weight training was considered weird and even dangerous. In 1935, while still in his twenties, he started a gym in an old office building in Oakland, California. He was the first to create the concept of the general-use fitness center that included not only the gym but also a juice bar and health-food store. His idea became the prototype for all the fitness centers to follow.

Years later, he wrote of the opposition he encountered. He said that "people thought I was a charlatan and a nut. The doctors were against me—they said that working out with weights would give people heart attacks and they would lose their sex drive."

In 1951, he began a local television show in San Francisco that went national in 1959. He used a white German shepherd named Happy to attract an audience by performing tricks. He had little money to start and used the simple props of a broomstick, a chair, and a rubber cord to demonstrate strength exercise. His most famous demonstrations were his fingertip push-ups. The show continued into the 1980s as he inspired a generation to choose physical fitness as a way of life.

At 60, he swam from Alcatraz Island to Fisherman's Wharf while handcuffed and towing a 1,000-pound boat. At 70, he repeated the swim, again handcuffed and towing 70 boats carrying 70 people. He died at 96 of pneumonia.

Jack Lalanne believed that fitness saved his life. He said he did not even like working out, but the health benefits were so great, he followed the program. He said it was worth it to look and feel so good.

Look at yourself. Are you fit? How do you feel? How do you look? Do you want to look and feel better? What are you willing to do about it?

First, consult your doctor and then start a fitness program, even if it only begins with a short walk. Jack would tell you to do it.

The Bible says, *"Do you not know that your bodies are temples of the Holy Spirit, who is in you, whom you have received from God? You are not your own;you were bought at a price. Therefore honor God with your bodies." (1 Corinthians 6:19-20)*

Treat the temple with respect.

31 - It's Not That Bad!

These are actual comments from people who knew him.

One man called him, "a half-breed..." and, "the greatest adventurer [not a compliment] in modern political history."

Another described him as, "part of the flotsam and jetsam of political drift thrown up on the beach."

A fellow worker said, "there seems to be some inclination...to believe that [he] will be a complete failure."

A man who had been acquainted with him for years wrote, "Perhaps he will win...Perhaps he won't. How anybody could expect him [to win], I don't know, in view of his unparalleled record of losing everything he puts his hand to."

A man who regularly worked with him said that he was a "terrible risk, and I cannot help feeling that [we] have been maneuvered into the most dangerous position..."

When he had time to think about it, the man just mentioned further said, "Seldom can [someone] have taken [a position] with the Establishment so dubious of the choice and so prepared to have it's doubts justified."

But this same man later wrote, "Within a fortnight [two weeks] all was changed."

The man so slandered by these, and many other, public and private attacks, became the leader, almost universally acclaimed, as "the man of the century." The one man who is credited as the single most important figure in saving the world from the dark night of Nazi terror and tyranny. This is the man who will always be remembered for asking the Parliament of Great Britain, in his first speech as Prime Minister, "You ask, what is our aim? I answer in one word: It is **victory**, victory at all costs..."

The road was not always easy for Winston Leonard Spencer Churchill. He was assailed by doubters and attacked by leaders. He was considered a fool and a failure, not to be trusted with great responsibility. He was also the warrior the world needed. He was, in the words of William Manchester, "the last lion."

The next time you are tempted to wilt under the pressure of negative pressure, remember Winston Churchill. The next time you are tempted to surrender to self-doubt, remember Winston Churchill. Things are not as bad as you think. You can still win. You can still conquer. You can still come out on top. All you have to do, to use another of Churchill's magnificent phrases, is "to never give up."

Joshua 1:9 says, "Be strong and courageous. Do not be afraid or discouraged, for the LORD your God is with you wherever you go." (HCSB)

It's not that bad. You can still win.

32 - Choose to Win

It started when George could not make it to the top of the stairs. He was 45 years old, enjoying a successful medical practice and smoking heavily. When he failed to reach the landing, he grabbed the railing and heaved air into his tortured lungs. As he waited to recover, he felt a wave of disgust. He realized that he had become everything he hated: an overweight tobacco-dependent man who was aging before his time.

The next two minutes changed his life forever. He was seized with a sudden vision of who he could still be. He decided to challenge his broken approach to life and launch a mission to transform his health. He became a runner.

He calculated that 26 loops around his back yard in Rumson, New Jersey, made one mile. He organized his daily routine into a fitness program, stopped smoking, and redirected his diet into more fruits and vegetables. Five years later, he ran a mile in 4 minutes and 47 seconds, which was the fastest time ever recorded by a 50-year-old. He became a regular contributor to Runner's World magazine; and he wrote Running and Being: The Total Experience, which became a New York Times bestseller.

The two-minute awakening on the stairway in his home led George Sheehan to a new world of health and purpose.

Do you need an awakening? Is your life all that you have hoped for? Are you standing on the stairs stunned by the realization that you are not the person you planned to be?

You have a God-given potential deep inside. There is a dream that stirs you and pushes you. As you stand on your stairway, that dream is seeking release.

The critical moment for Dr. Sheehan came when he realized that his choices had produced a result he didn't want. He had walked his road to ruin, and only he could take the exit. He, a track star in college, had thrown away the discipline and training principles that had been proven to work to try another plan that had failed.

The big questions for you right now are these: Is your life working? Are your finances growing? Are you following a plan that will get you where you want to go? If not, why not?

There are reasons people succeed. Achievement is not based on luck. Happiness does not happen by mistake.

The Bible says in Deuteronomy 11:26–28, *"See, I am setting before you today a blessing and a curse—the blessing if you obey the commands of the Lord your God that I am giving you today; the curse if you disobey the commands of the Lord your God and turn from the way that I command you today by following other gods, which you have not known." (NIV)*

33 - Ha Ha Ha

Why did the chicken cross the road? Because he wanted to get to the other side.

We all like to laugh. Humor lifts the heart and lubricates relationships. But it actually does more than that.

In 1995, researchers at the Loma Linda University School of Medicine arranged for 10 students to watch a video of a comedian named Gallagher smash watermelons with a sledgehammer. It was a very funny video. The researchers found that there was a measurable decrease in stress hormones (epinephrine and dopamine) and a marked increase in endorphins (the body's feel-good painkillers) in the blood samples of every one of the 10 subjects.

Even more positive results were recorded in the immune systems of the students. These included:

1. Increased levels of gamma interferon, a hormone that activates the immune system and fights viruses.

2. Increased amounts of T-cells, which help the body resist illness.

3. Increased Complement 3 (C3) protein levels, which help antibodies kill infections and eliminate damaged cells so new healthy ones can grow.

4. Increased NK cells (Natural killer cells) that protect the body from foreign cells, cancer cells, and cells infected by viruses.

Let me suggest the following:

1. Lighten up! Don't take everything (especially yourself) so seriously.
2. Read a funny book or watch a funny movie at least twice a month. Your immune system will thank you.
3. Learn to see the natural humor in everyday situations. Look around. If you see people, you will soon see something funny.

One of my favorite Bible verses says, *"A cheerful heart is good medicine." (Proverbs 17:22 NIV)*

Laugh at something today.

34 - Curiosity

He was born in Lichfield, Staffordshire, England, on September 18, 1709. When he died in 1784, he was the most famous man in the nation. Even today, over 1800 of his quotes circulate on the Internet.

He was physically ugly and grossly overweight. He walked with a lurching shuffle that resembled a great bear forcing its way through the woods. Even with his bulk, he was surprisingly strong: a boxer who was described as "terrifyingly good."

King George III paid him a stipend of 300 pounds a year (a typical worker made only one pound a year) to, as Boris Johnson writes, "simply exist." Tourists regularly visited his home at Johnson's Court just off Fleet Street, hoping for a glimpse of him. When he died, Edmund Burke (the greatest political philosopher of the age) was a pallbearer. He was buried at Westminster Abbey (site of the famous wedding of Prince Charles and Princess Diana) and was honored by monuments at St. Paul's Cathedral and Lichfield Cathedral. The Sunday after he died, almost every congregation of the Church of England heard a sermon that featured his life.

Samuel Johnson was not an athlete, scientist, inventor, politician, or explorer. So what made him so special? He was hugely curious about everything, and he dedicated his life to understanding and explaining life to everyone he could.

His greatest accomplishment was to organize the first dictionary of the English language. It took forty Frenchmen 55 years to compose the first dictionary of French. It took The Accamedia della Crusca, collectively, 20 years to produce the first dictionary of Italian. It took Johnson only nine years to build the first English dictionary, and he did it alone. He wrote 40,000 of the entries himself. When he was challenged by a woman who pointed out a mistake and then asked him why he had been wrong, he replied, "Ignorance, Madam, ignorance."

He was considered the most fascinating conversationalist of his era and was in constant demand at the best dinner parties. He loved people, food, and family. He was devoted to his wife and his cat, Hodge. No one was more popular.

His most famous quote reveals much about what made him so exceptional. He once said, "When you are tired of London, you are tired of life...." His massive curiosity about everything kept him intellectually young and made him loved by all who knew him.

What about you? Do you have a vibrant curiosity about life? Do you hunt for new and exciting information? Are you fascinated by people? Are you young in mind and heart?

Why don't you make it a point to learn something new each week? You may be surprised at the result.

Turn on your mind. Keep learning. Stay young all your life. The Bible says in Ecclesiastes 3:6, *"[There is] a time to search."* (NIV)

Keep your curiosity alive.

35 - What's in a Name?

I know a man who calls himself, "Battery Bob". I have always liked his name because it makes him easy to remember and the word "battery" lets me think of positive energy.

I don't know how he got the name but it certainly makes him stand out.

Sometimes you give a nick-name to a friend to help identify something about them. In college we called the older student who monitored our residence hall, "tyrant", even though his name was Frank. He wasn't actually a tyrant but the name fit, in a fun way, because he was always checking up on us. I had two nick-names in college. I started as "mad dog" and finished as "the rose." Don't ask.

Groups of animals are sometimes labeled in odd ways.

There is, for example:

- A shrewdness of apes.
- A cloud of bats.
- A sloth of bears.
- A wake of buzzards.
- A bask of crocodiles.
- A murder of crows.
- A congregation of eagles.
- A seething of eels.
- A tower of giraffes.
- A bloat of hippopotamuses.
- A cackle of hyenas.
- A mischief of mice.
- A prickle of porcupines.
- And a rhumba of rattlesnakes.

There are always names and names matter. If you want to make a great impression on someone, remember their name. A person's name is the most powerful word in their vocabulary. When you learn and remember someone's name you show that you value and respect them. You stand out as a leader when you call people by name.

Let me suggest that:

1. You focus when you meet someone. It helps to say their name just after you meet. Some studies say you should repeat the name at least three times.
2. Use rhymes and "sound-a-like" words that help you remember. For example, when you meet a Bill, think, "I climb the hill with Bill", or something similar.

What's in a name? Great possibilities, when you remember and use it. Even God had Adam give each animal a name. *"He [God] brought them [the animals] to the man to see what he would name them; and whatever the man called each living creature, that was its name."* (Genesis 2:19 NIV)

Names are that important. Become known for knowing people's names. They will love you for it.

36 - Ideas

In 2009 the British government chose key examples of memorable British design to be featured on postage stamps.

The list included:

1. The polyprop chair.
2. The miniskirt.
3. The red phone booth.
4. The Concorde supersonic jet.
5. The Mini automobile.

You are probably familiar with the final four, but do you know what the polyprop chair is and why it was selected?

Robin Day invented the chair in 1962, and its design quickly spread all over the world. He made it of a "molded polypropylene shell fastened to an enameled bent tubular steel base."

Journalist Bruce Weber of the New York Times called it "comfortable, durable, inexpensive, light-weight, easy to clean and easy to store." The original design has sold over 14 million units, and 500,000 new ones are still sold every year.

One more thing made it the most popular chair ever invented: It was the first chair that was stackable, which meant that churches, schools, offices, auditoriums, and private homes could store as many as they needed and pull them out when required. It was a simple idea of pure genius.

Treasure your ideas because you don't know what an idea can produce. You can never predict the future of a good idea.

Let me suggest:

1. Keep a notebook (or electronic device capable of recording) available at all times. You never know when inspiration will strike.
2. Write (or record) EVERY idea. You will usually forget unless you note the actual thought.
3. Do not dismiss an idea because it seems too crazy or simple. It may lead to something significant.

It is wise to look for good ideas. The Bible says that wisdom *"is more profitable than silver and yields better returns than gold." (Proverbs 3:14 NIV)*

37 - Escape

In 1963 a film was released in both the United States and Europe. It was based on the largest break-out of allied prisoners of war from a German prison camp during all of World War II.

The actual escape took place in 1944 when 250 prisoners escaped from Stalag Luft III in what is now Poland. The incident caused shock waves throughout Nazi Germany because the camp had been designed to be "escape-proof" with the newest and best (or so they thought) security technology ever devised.

The 1963 film *The Great Escape* starred Steve McQueen, James Garner, and Richard Attenborough. Attenborough played RAF officer Roger Bartlett, who masterminded the escape by organizing the prisoners. In one scene, he inspired the men by telling them that he was proud to be imprisoned with "the greatest escape artists in the world."

Movie goers must have been inspired as well because the movie, which cost $11,744 to produce, went on to gross $3.8 million (a large sum at that time) to become one of the biggest hits of the year.

Raymond Flannery Jr., PhD, writing from the Harvard Medical School, says studies of the healthiest people (those with the lowest levels of distress and disease) show that all enjoy some form of daily relaxation. Dr. Flannery calls this "active relaxation"; and to be effective, it should last at least 15 minutes. He writes that this time-out should be a complete escape from the regular routines and responsibilities of the day. He further states that this period should be stress-free and filled with something you truly enjoy, such as listening to music, walking outside, or looking at photos of people and scenes that make you happy.

Leonardo da Vinci said, "Every now and then go away, even briefly, have a little relaxation, for when you come back to your work your judgment will be surer: since to remain constantly at work will cause you to lose power…."

Let me suggest:

1. Escape for at least 15 minutes twice a day. The first time will refresh you and anticipating the second will energize you.
2. Prepare for your special escape: Have music or a book with positive statements ready. In addition to reading exciting Bible verses, I enjoy carrying around travel brochures of places I want to visit so I can look and be inspired. I even carry trail maps of places I want to hike so I can imagine the experience. You can do the same with everything from golf courses to beaches. Do what works.

Jesus said in Mark 6:31, *"Come with me by yourselves to a quiet place and get some rest." (NIV)*

Enjoy your escape.

38 - A Worthy Goal

Eugene Goldwasser is a hero you have probably never heard of.

He was born in Brooklyn on October 14, 1922. When his father's clothing business failed during the Depression, the family moved to Kansas City, Missouri, where he attended high school. He entered a small community college and then transferred to the University of Chicago on a scholarship, eventually earning a doctorate in biochemistry.

In 1906, two French researchers originated the idea that something in human blood caused the production of healthy blood cells, but they could not find proof. In 1956, Dr. Goldwasser decided to locate the mysterious substance. He thought the search would take a few months, but it stretched into 20 years. He eventually isolated a protein he called *erythropoietin*, now known as EPO. It is the trigger that tells the body to produce red blood cells, which carry oxygen to the tissues of the body.

All this matters because EPO is now mass-produced and given to patients all over the world to cure anemia. This is a breakthrough because, as Andrew Pollack writes, "Most people undergoing kidney dialysis now receive EPO, helping relieve them of severe anemia ... [and] Many cancer patients also get the drug to combat anemia caused by chemotherapy." Dr. Gary Toback, a friend and colleague of Dr. Goldwasser, said, "It just continually delighted him that the work he did ended up having an impact on patients."

Dr. Goldwasser once wrote that he had no idea the results would be so useful, but he always seemed to believe that his pursuit of the elusive protein was a worthy goal. It took him 20 years, but he never gave up. What about you? Do you have worthy goals? Are you in hot pursuit of great results? Are you striving for something that can bless and help people?

Let me suggest the following:

1. Make a list of 5 worthy goals that excite you personally. Remember that it is OK to start small.
2. Pray for God's guidance then pick one and make a plan to accomplish it.
3. Repeat the process. When you have finished one goal, return to the list and do the process again.
4. Keep going until you become an expert at doing good.

The Bible says, *"Whatever you do, do it all for the glory of God."* *(1 Corinthians 10:31 NIV)*

39 - The Right Gift

Lew was well liked by everyone who met him.

He was born in Edinburgh, Scotland, the son of a lighthouse engineer. Because of his father's influence, he entered Edinburgh University to study engineering, but changed to law, graduated, and was called to the bar as a lawyer in 1875. He was restless, eventually living in France, the United States, and the island of Samoa in the South Pacific.

He found that he was more interested in stories than the practice of law, so he began to write fiction. He tried short stories, children's literature, and poetry. In the 1880s, he met a one-legged poet named W.E. Henley who inspired him to create a one-legged rascally pirate. He named him Long John Silver and made him the center of an adventure story he published in 1883 called *Treasure Island*. He followed the worldwide success of that novel with *Kidnapped* (1886), *Strange Case of Dr. Jekyll and Mr. Hyde* (1886), and *The Master of Ballantrae* (1889).

Robert Louis Stevenson moved to Samoa in 1890, with his wife Fanny, in hopes that the tropical climate would help cure his tuberculosis. He was loved by the Samoans, who called him *Tusitala*, which means "teller of stories." His condition worsened, and he died on the island on December 3, 1894. Before he died, he prepared a will that left an unusual gift to someone he barely knew. He instructed his executor to contact a young child who had once told him that since her birthday was on December 25 (Christmas Day), she was always a bit sad because she only received one set of presents. He directed that the child be told that "Lew" had given her his birthday of November 13 as a special gift so she would always have a separate birthday to celebrate.

The right gift can make a special difference in someone's life.

When you give a gift that fits the person, that gift becomes even more meaningful.

My daughter, Allison, has the gift of friendship. She spends time carefully researching and planning each gift she gives. Because of this, those gifts help create a deeper level of connection and relationship. To Allison, there is no such thing as a casual gift. (She learned this from her mother, Amy, who is a genius at gift-giving and who works throughout every year to select just the right gifts.)

Let me suggest:

1. Make a list of everyone to whom you plan to give a gift (small or large) this year. Spend some time thinking of the right gift for each person. Add the right gift to the list.
2. Make gift-giving an expression of genuine caring for the other person. Make the gifts matter. Remember that this level of thoughtfulness is more important than the price of the gift.

The Bible says that *"every good and perfect gift is from above, coming down from the Father." (James 1:17 NIV)* Of course, God's perfect gift is His Son, our Savior Jesus Christ; and it is good to remember that God loves to give His children gifts. You can do the same to the people in your life. Always try to give the right gift.

40 - Thanks for the Memories

Have you ever heard of Ruth Hunt?

She started selling candy, based on her private recipes, in 1921. She encountered such success that she expanded, opening a full candy factory in Mt. Sterling, Kentucky, in 1930. She eventually sold 70 varieties of candy, but her most popular confections were Cream Candy and Bourbon Balls. Her recipes are still prepared with the highest quality ingredients: real whipping cream, dairy butter, and fresh milk. The Ruth Hunt Candy Company carries on her commitment to top standards today. Her famous Cream Candy (also known as "pulled candy") is still prepared in hand-stirred copper kettles and cooled on huge old marble slabs.

Ruth Hunt's best-known creation is the Blue Monday candy bar. It is made of cream candy covered in extra rich, dark chocolate. It was inspired by a visit to the factory by a church pastor who asked if the factory store had any type of candy that would be good for an enjoyable experience on a "blue Monday."

The White House once ordered 80 pounds of Ruth Hunt candies for use as Christmas gifts. Their Cream Candy has been featured in an article in the *New York Times*; and in 1993, Ruth Hunt Candy became the official candy of Churchill Downs and the Kentucky Derby.

Since childhood, my favorite candy has been (and still is) cream candy. I have happy memories of helping my mother, aunts, and various cousins make homemade cream candy. We didn't have giant copper kettles, but we always used small marble slabs because, as my mother explained, "You just can't make real cream candy without a marble slab." The candy would come out blistering hot. My cousins and I would cover our arms with butter to guard against the heat and pull the candy into long, thin strips. The mothers would then lay the candy on the slab, cut the strips with scissors into bite-sized morsels, and then leave it to cool. The completed candy always tasted fantastic.

Because of the labor-intensive nature of cream candy, I buy the candy now from the Ruth Hunt Company. My favorite is the one covered in dark chocolate. My son, Jonathan, has given me stacks of Blue Monday bars as Christmas gifts over the past two years. They have been one of my happiest gifts.

The only thing that is better than the warm memories aroused by cream candy is the candy itself.

Let me suggest:

1. Make special memories with your family and friends. Savor time together.
2. Write a brief description—add pictures if possible—when you have had an especially happy experience. Chronicle everything in a journal of happy memories.
3. Consider making something you enjoy together (like making pulled cream candy) an ongoing tradition.

Use your positive memories to enhance your current relationships. The Bible says in Philippians 1:3, *"I thank my God every time I remember you." (NIV)*

41 - A Chocolate Dream

Milton grew up in Hockersville, Pennsylvania, a small town, surrounded by farms and fields.

When he was 19, he started his first business, storing and selling candy, but it soon failed. Because of his love of candy, he decided to become a traveling salesman, selling candy over several states. He learned to make caramels in Denver and developed direct selling techniques while selling candy on the street in New York City.

Milton settled in Lancaster, Pennsylvania, where he established a new candy company that specialized in the caramels he had learned to make in Denver. In 1893, he traveled to Chicago where he met a German businessman who had invented a chocolate-making machine. He bought one of the units, eventually dropped other candy items, and focused on chocolate. (He sold his caramel company for $1 million and used the money to build a chocolate factory in South Central Pennsylvania.) Together with a few trusted workers, he locked himself in a room and labored to create the perfect milk chocolate recipe. He succeeded. His first new chocolate bar was marketed in 1925 and called Mr. Goodbar. This was followed by Krackel and a long, rectangular bar he named after himself, the Hershey Bar.

Milton Hershey insisted on strict quality control and the best ingredients. To guarantee a top-quality sugar supply, he developed his own sugar plantation in Cuba. He once said in response to a question about his success, "Give them quality, that's the best kind of advertising in the world."

Hershey also had a deep commitment to the people who worked for him. He was devoted to the welfare of the families of his employees. To give them a positive living environment, he created a town around the chocolate factory. He opened a competition to select a name for the town, but the winner, "Hersheyoko," was vetoed by the United States Postal Service. The town eventually became simply "Hershey."

Milton was famous for his bold risk-taking and entrepreneurial vision, but it should be remembered that his determination to create the perfect milk chocolate recipe was the cornerstone of his success.

What are the lessons you can learn from Milton Snavely Hershey?

1. Focus on something you passionately love. Milton Hershey loved candy, which led him to fall in love with chocolate.
2. Develop the skills to help accomplish your goal. Mr. Hershey learned to make his own caramels, which eventually made him $1 million in 1920s money. He also learned direct marketing skills on the tough streets of New York.
3. Take care of the people who help you. Tell your team (including your family) how much you appreciate and value them. Show them your commitment by what you do for them.

The Bible says in Proverbs 24:3–4, *"By wisdom a house is built, and through understanding it is established; through knowledge its rooms are filled with rare and beautiful treasures."* (NIV)

Milton Hershey built his success with wisdom and knowledge; so can you.

42 - Look Within

His name was originally Zantar but was later changed to Tublat Zan. He was a young, remarkably athletic young man, who spoke French, English, Dutch, German, Swahili and Bantu, as well as ancient Greek, Latin and Mayan. Today, he is one of the most famous people in the world, with name recognition in almost every country. His career is followed in 26 books (and those are just the official ones), and he has starred in 89 movies. He is known today by his eventual name, Tarzan.

Edgar Rice Burroughs published his first Tarzan story, *Tarzan of the Apes*, in *All-Story* magazine in October 1912. The story was so popular he reissued it in book form in 1914. The character was so well-received he was featured in his first movie in 1918, played by Elmo Lincoln. He inspired Jane Goodall, famous British chimpanzee researcher, to pursue a world-renowned career in primate studies. Goodall once said that she had believed, since she first read the Tarzan stories as a young girl, that she would have made a much better wife for Tarzan than Jane.

The famous Tarzan yell (the "victory cry of a bull ape") was first heard from the lips of Johnny Weissmuller in the 1932 film Tarzan the Ape-Man. Weissmuller was an Olympic gold medal swimmer and was picked for the part partially because of his physical appearance. Weissmuller was also trained in the European art of yodeling and used his training to create the unforgettable yell. Although this account is in dispute, Weissmuller, his son, and even his Tarzan co-star, Maureen O'Sullivan, all claimed that the yell was Weissmuller's authentic creation.

The most important lesson from this is that when something as critical as the "yell" was needed in the film, Weissmuller proved that he already had what was needed within him.

What do you have within you that could make a difference in your life? What skills, talents, or insights do you already have that, if developed, could blow the lid off your future?

1. List everything you are good at doing, whether it seems significant or not.
2. Take that list and choose three things you can develop to improve your chances for success.

The Bible says in Proverbs 14:8, *"The wisdom of the prudent is to give thought to their ways." (NIV)*

Ask God to help you "give thought to your ways." You may be happily surprised at what you find.

43 - Sit Up Straight

I once spent part of an hour eating chocolate chip cookies with Ronald Reagan.

I was on a speaking circuit with Reagan for a portion of the first year following his presidency. Reagan and I would share the platform at conventions. He was always bright, courteous and supportive. He consistently made us feel special. His blend of leadership and humility sparked loyalty and appreciation from all of us who worked with him.

On one occasion Reagan asked me and two others if we liked American football. When we said yes, he proceeded to teach us his favorite play from his days as a collegiate football player. He even had us line up and run the actual play, even though we were in a holding room at a convention center. It was great and memorable fun.

In addition to Reagan's unusual graciousness as a human being, I also noticed his confident posture. He was in his seventies but still stood and sat, ramrod straight. His physical posture was a compelling expression of his leadership abilities. He still regularly rode horses and his fitness helped project his confidence.

Dr. David Imrie, M.D., an occupational medicine specialist, says that, "Posture is not solely the manifestation of physical balance. It's also an expression of mental balance."

Dr. Robert Cooper writes, "Research suggests that how you sit and stand may exert a powerful influence not only on how rapidly you age but also on your mind and mood … slouching or hunching over in your chair creates 10–15 times as much pressure on your lower back as does sitting up straight … when you're slumped … it also restricts your breathing and impedes circulation. But here's the key: Sitting and standing with upright, relaxed posture is a choice you make—or fail to make—every day of your life."

It seems that as gravity pulls you down, it is better for you to fight back with correct posture.

The list today is very short and very simple:

1. Sit up straight.
2. Stand tall.

The Bible says that *"Jesus grew in wisdom and stature."* (Luke 2:52 NIV) You can do the same.

44 - A Humble Heart

He played polo and rode horses well enough to briefly qualify as an extra in a cowboy movie for Warner Brothers Studio. He loved Hollywood and had wanted a career in entertainment since he was a young man.

He was born in Chicago in 1901, the fourth son of a farmer who moved the family to Missouri in 1906. The family moved again when he was 12 and settled in Kansas City. He eventually returned to Chicago and enrolled in the Chicago Academy of Fine Arts, where he studied illustration. He supported himself by working as a night watchman and as a postman. When World War I erupted, he lied about his age and served in France as an ambulance driver for the Red Cross. After the war, he returned to Kansas City and worked as an illustrator.

While he was working at the Newman Laugh-O-Gram company, he kept a pet mouse named Mortimer. His wife didn't like the name, so he changed it to Mickey and decided to draw a cartoon based on the small rodent. His creation was introduced to the world on November 18, 1928. The mouse became hugely popular and formed the foundation of an entertainment empire. He eventually won 26 Academy Awards for multiple animated and live films and opened the first themed entertainment complex in Anaheim, California, in 1956. He used his family name and called it Disneyland.

Walt Disney became a towering legend in entertainment. He generated hundreds of millions of dollars and was one of the best-known and most-loved celebrities in the world by the time he died on December 15, 1966. But even with his phenomenal success, he retained a simple humility. He never took himself too seriously and was always grateful for the privileges he enjoyed. He was devoted to his wife, Lillian, and daughter, Sharon. Once, when he was asked what it was like being such a giant celebrity, he said that being a celebrity, "doesn't seem to keep fleas off our dogs, and if being a celebrity won't give one an advantage over a couple of fleas, then I guess there can't be much in being a celebrity after all." His humble heart protected him from the temptations and potential disasters of the typical celebrity lifestyle.

Check yourself:

1. Watch your reactions. Be aware whether you are overly sensitive and easily offended. It may be your ego showing.
2. Monitor your conversations. Try to focus on and listen to the other person; don't talk mostly about yourself. Ask a trusted friend to tell you the truth about how you work with other people. People will be more likely to help you when you show humility.
3. Show gratitude for your blessings and accomplishments. Acknowledge God's help and the support of other people in what you've done.

God blesses a humble heart. The Bible says that *"humility comes before honor."* (Proverbs 15:33 NIV) And to *"humble yourselves, therefore, under God's mighty hand, that he may lift you up in due time.* (1 Peter 5:6 NIV)

45 - Snow Days

It has been snowing heavily for the past eight hours, and the temperature has dropped 10 degrees in less than an hour. The forecast calls for more snow and a low of 5 degrees Fahrenheit this evening. We are having a snow day in Kentucky.

Bernard Mergen in his book *Snow In America* writes, "At 9–12 kilometers (30,000 to 40,000 feet) above us, temperatures cool to -60 degrees C (-76 degrees F), a level rarely reached even at the poles…. Water vapor condenses and becomes liquid in cold, saturated air. It freezes around some nuclei at just below 0 degrees C…. As they descend toward earth, these ice crystals go through a process called sublimation—transforming from solid to gaseous to solid without liquefying and growing from invisible particles to aggregations of crystals we call snowflakes." It is an accumulation of these snowflakes that creates snowstorms and snow days.

According to the National Weather Service, the largest snowstorm ever recorded in the United States was March 11–12, 1888. This monster storm dropped 40–50 inches of snow on the eastern United States, and drifts of 50 feet were documented. The biggest snowstorm I have ever experienced was in Gatlinburg, Tennessee, in March 1993. I was speaking to a convention of 5,000 people. On Friday, it was 72 degrees Fahrenheit. By the next day, we were buried in 37 inches of snow, and the temperature was 18 degrees below zero Fahrenheit. Amy, Allison, and I were stranded for five days.

My first reaction to today's storm was a determination to keep going. I had made a list of priorities the night before, and I had decided to ignore the weather and do the list. I had finished several items when I stopped at a park to walk in the snow, and I realized I was missing a magical opportunity. I had been given an unexpected break. My family was home, and I had absolutely nowhere I had to go. I had been given a "snow day." So I returned home, built a roaring fire, and settled in for a winter interlude with the people I love most. As I write this, I feel no guilt, because, after all, it is a snow day.

Sometimes the best thing you can do with an unexpected break in the action is to embrace the moment and enjoy your surprise gift.

The Bible says in Ecclesiastes 3:5 that there is a time *"to embrace." (NIV)* Maybe you need to embrace your unplanned interruption; it may be just what you need.

46 - Courage

Aerial combat was something new and daring in the First World War. Most pilots started each day not knowing if they would return alive. Those who survived were measured by the victories they won. It was so challenging to defeat an enemy aircraft that only five victories qualified a pilot as an "ace." One American, however, was so good at downing enemy planes that he became the only American "ace of aces." He scored 26 victories, and his style of attack was so ferocious that he became a legend, even to the Germans. He was a race car driver from Columbus, Ohio, named Eddie Rickenbacker.

Eddie developed a reputation for fearlessness, but the truth was far different. He would fly calm and controlled in combat but be shaken and drained when he returned.

A reporter once asked him about this and tossed in the comment that Eddie seemed to have no fear in the air. Rickenbacker's reply became famous as a definition of true courage. He looked at the reporter and explained that courage was not the absence of fear; it was the decision to pursue the goal in spite of the fear. It is only possible to have courage when faced with fear because courage is the choice to overcome fear. Rickenbacker then said that, of course, he fought fear in combat; he just chose to win because the mission was more important.

You can overcome fear if your purpose is great enough. You can choose courage when you focus on the decision to win. Don't be embarrassed at the feelings of fear. It is what you do with those feelings that matters. Concentrate on your purpose; lock in on your goal, and fight through the fear. You may be surprised at what you can accomplish.

Remember the following:

1. Fear is an emotion, not a reality.
2. Courage is a choice. It is in your power to make that choice.
3. "Facts don't count," says a friend of mine, "if your dream is big enough." He doesn't mean facts are meaningless, but what may look like insurmountable facts may just be excuses. You can decide what to do with those excuses.

You are who you choose to be. Choose to be a man or woman of courage. Choose the courage to get things done.

The Bible says, *"Be strong and courageous." (Joshua 1:6 NIV)*

47 - Reading

I first met Charlie backstage at a convention in Atlanta. He and I were both scheduled to speak during the evening program, and we were waiting together in a holding area. One of the coordinators of the event introduced us, and to my surprise, Charlie grabbed me in a happy hug. He was a big man and easily lifted me off my feet. When I returned to earth, he smiled and hugged me again. I had just met Charlie "Tremendous" Jones. It was the beginning of an enjoyable friendship.

Charlie was a gifted motivational speaker who often had his audiences convulsed with laughter. He was known for doing the unexpected, and people never knew what outrageous stunt he might perform next. He was famous for calling people out of the audience and including them in his act. Everyone soon learned not to sit on the front row.

Charlie began as a hyper-successful insurance salesman, developed into a sales trainer, and finally moved into motivational seminars. He became one of the most popular speakers in that arena. Though he was recognized for his communication skills, he was also famous for his determination to encourage everyone he encountered to be a committed reader. He invented a phrase that is still used today: "Leaders are readers and readers are leaders." He believed that and pushed it at every opportunity.

The noted British author Peter Ackroyd says books are "the silent pleasure ... the nurse of daydreams and reflections, the mistress of the passions, the instigator of adventure and change. And ... literally change lives." That may be a bit flowery, but the fact is that reading opens doors like nothing else can.

Reading provides a shortcut to experience. You do not have the time to live the lifetime of another person. But when you read

10 biographies, you have taken a shortcut into the life experiences of 10 people, and you did it in days or weeks, not years. Reading exposes you to ideas and thoughts that can expand your mind to greater levels. It gives you amazing insight into people and why they do what they do. Reading takes you to places you cannot physically visit, and it teaches you skills that can improve your odds for happiness and success. God even chose to communicate Himself through a book, the Bible. Brain science even reveals that parts of your brain are only stimulated by reading. Wow! Reading may be one of your most effective life tools.

If you are not a reader, start with something simple and fun. Start with fiction, then move to subjects that teach you what you want to learn. Learn to enjoy the process. It may pay bigger dividends than you ever realized. This is not a boring school assignment; this is a way to enhance your life.

The Bible says in Ecclesiastes 12:12, *"Of making many books there is no end." (NIV)* And speaking of Jesus Christ, it also says, *"In the beginning was the Word, and the Word was with God, and the Word was God. The Word became flesh and made his dwelling among us." (John 1:1, 14 NIV)* It all started with "the Word."

Readers are leaders and leaders are readers. Thank you, Charlie.

48 - An Environment of Harmony

He was a genius with a troubled private life. His personal history included scandal, multiple affairs, divorce, and a wild ax murder (not by him) that took the lives of seven people. He rose to the heights of national popularity and dropped to the depths of rejection more than once. His professional peers voted him the best ever in their field, and today he is recognized as the ultimate success in his industry. Over 60 years after his death, people still pay to see his works.

In 1991, the American Institute of Architects selected Frank Lloyd Wright as the greatest architect of all time. During his career, he developed 1,000 original designs and completed 532 homes and buildings. Fallingwater (a residence built in 1935), in the Laurel Highlands of southwestern Pennsylvania, is considered by most experts as the greatest-known example of American architecture. This design is only rivaled by the stunning Guggenheim Art Museum in New York City. Wright based the Guggenheim on the look of a sea shell and worked on the structure for 16 years.

Wright called his design approach "organic architecture" and did everything to create a sense of harmony between human beings and their environment. The best example of this is Fallingwater, which was constructed as a private home. The house is built over a natural waterfall and is so peaceful and beautiful it was made a National Historic Landmark in 1966; it is also on the Smithsonian list of the 28 places to see before you die. Everything about it is based on the idea of harmony.

Brain science recognizes that order is important for a sense of well-being. The brain places the world in mental categories that help organize its response to the outside. When you live in clutter and disorganization, you experience disharmony and unease. It is difficult to feel calm and peaceful in a disjointed and unharmonious setting. Wright was right: Organic architecture, based on order and harmony, helps to give you clarity and focus. This is why you immediately feel better when you clean your closet or clear your desk.

Let me suggest:

1. Pick a room in your home to declutter and organize. How do you feel?
2. Simplify and reorganize your weekly calendar. Does your focus and attitude improve?
3. Create more harmony with nature in your living arrangements: Open the shades. Sit outside (weather permitting). Place fresh flowers where you can easily see them.

Remember that when God made the first man and woman, He put them in a garden.

The Bible says in 1 Corinthians 14:33, *"For God is not a God of disorder but of peace." (NIV)*

49 - Waiting for Results

MCA Records originally said they were not interested in the song. They thought it might offend some people, or worse yet, not sell. The song's author disagreed and decided to fight for his work to be published and released, regardless of the negative opinions of his record agency. That's how it all started.

The songwriter penned his piece after an unarmed Korean commercial passenger jet was shot down by Russian fighter jets after the plane accidentally wandered into Russian air space. This happened on September 1, 1983. Two hundred sixty-nine people died, including 63 Americans. While the country rocked with shock and outrage, this country music performer decided to do something in response. (He was the son of a career Navy musician. He had spent years struggling in an obscure Las Vegas act and had finally broken out and experienced success with six country song hits in a row.)

The singer wrote a song that expressed his love and support for America, and he took it to Jerry Crutchfield, his producer. Jerry liked the song but was unable to persuade MCA executives to release it, because they considered it too sentimental. The author then recorded a demo, flew to Los Angeles (at his own expense), and presented it personally to Irving Azoff, the president of MCA. Azoff, impressed by the artist's commitment and persistence, agreed to include the song as part of the singer's upcoming album, but did not agree to release it as a single—which meant the song would probably fade and die because only singles received radio play time.

When Azoff heard a preview of the new album, he was so touched by the song he changed his mind and released it as a single. It climbed to No. 7 on the country charts but was considered a failure because several of the singer's previous songs had all reached No. 1. The singer's career was so damaged (in the opinion of the MCA executives) that it took two years for him to recover.

The song was largely forgotten in the music industry, but something strange happened in grassroots America. The song began to be played by amateur musicians and semiprofessional bands across America, with an unexpected result. The song was so popular it became an unofficial national anthem. It was heard and sung in churches, civic halls, and music clubs. Soon the song became part of common culture, learned and loved by millions. When the terrorist attack occurred on September 11, 2001, the nation was ready for the song; and the song was ready for the nation. That number, by a determined country singer, developed into an expression of the national heart, and remains so today.

I'm sure even Lee Greenwood was surprised by the extraordinary success of "God Bless the USA."

Sometimes you need to wait for your results. The conclusion may be delayed, but success can still happen. In the Bible, God told David he would be king. Instead, he became an outcast and outlaw. It took 13 years before God's promise was fulfilled. God told Joseph at around age 15 that he would be a ruler, and it took 15 years of faith and preparation for the prediction to come true.

What are you waiting for? If it is part of God's plan for you, it will happen. The results may be delayed, but that doesn't mean they are not coming.

The Bible says, *"Blessed are all who wait for him!" (Isaiah 30:18 NIV)*

50 - Giggles

On May 15, 1963, astronaut Gordon Cooper was launched into space atop the Atlas rocket *Faith 7*. His mission was to travel 600,000 miles in a day and a half by orbiting the earth 22 times, tripling the previous American orbital record. It was a simple assignment that turned out to be not so simple.

The first eighteen orbits were uneventful. Cooper took a nap (he was the first human in history to sleep in space), performed a few experiments with weightlessness, took pictures of the earth, and ate several cubes of condensed peanut butter. As orbit 19 started, the unthinkable happened: The module began to fall out of its trajectory; and the ship's main electrical system shorted out, cutting off the cooling and oxygen purification systems, which caused a dangerous buildup of carbon dioxide in the cabin. Cooper decided to begin an immediate return to earth, but then the gyroscopes, which helped guide the vessel, stopped working.

NASA was monitoring the situation and contacted Cooper by radio just as the gyroscopes failed. When asked for his evaluation, Cooper calmly said, in an extraordinary understatement, "Things are beginning to stack up a little." On his twentieth orbit, the astronaut experienced a total system failure that left him "on a dying ship." His only hope was to engage a manual steering system and guide the ship back to earth. However, the manual system had never been used or even tested by anyone, and if it was not handled with precision, the ship would either burn up on reentering the atmosphere or crash on the surface of the planet. There was absolutely no margin for error. None. To make matters worse, Cooper was already dizzy with the effects of carbon dioxide poisoning.

As Cooper entered the atmosphere, he lost all communications and had to steer while battling the intense heat as well as the carbon dioxide poisoning. He endured this for fifteen agonizing minutes then manually released the parachutes, keeping the module on the only possible course angle for a successful touchdown. He guided the stricken ship to a perfect sea landing only four miles from the aircraft carrier, *USS Kearsarge*, sent to rescue him. He had done what no one, before or since, had done: He had safely landed an instrument-dead, powerless spacecraft and lived to fly again.

It is obvious that certain factors were critical to Cooper's survival. His training, his confidence, and his grace under pressure were all key elements. But one more (surprising) factor gives a clue to why he performed so well. He kept a positive sense of humor throughout the entire ordeal. At one tense moment, as every system failed, he told Mission Control that he had lost all critical operations but then added, "Other than that, things are fine." It is hard to tell from the flight recordings, but he may have actually giggled after he spoke.

Don't underestimate the power of a sense of humor. When Linda Henman interviewed 50 former Viet Nam prisoners of war, she found that most of them survived because of two things: faith in God and a healthy sense of humor. They had made jokes about their experiences while they were having them! John McCain still jokes about the crash that injured him and led to his capture. In an explanation of what happened, he says with a laugh, "I stopped a missile with my aircraft."

Learn to laugh at your situation. It may be the boost you need to win.

The Bible says in Proverbs 15:15, "*The cheerful heart has a continual feast.*"*(NIV)*

51 - Zest

Patrick Leigh Fermor was described by the BBC as "a cross between Indiana Jones, James Bond, and Graham Greene." When he was in his 90s, Anthony Lane, in a profile piece in the *New Yorker*, wrote, "If you think you can match him ouzo for ouzo, on a back street in Athens, you'd better think again." He sounds like the fictional character, who in a current TV commercial, is called "the most interesting man in the world." So, who is Patrick Leigh Fermor?

He joined the Irish Guards at the beginning of World War II and was considered so exceptional that he was selected for the Special Operations Executive (SOE), a specialized unit created by Winston Churchill to "wage war by unconventional means." He was a remarkable linguist whose fluency in modern Greek led to his assignment to direct the resistance to the Nazis in the Aegean region. He lived disguised as a shepherd for 18 months in Crete. He then surprised the German occupiers by kidnapping the German commander, escaping his pursuers, and delivering the commander to British authorities in Egypt. He received the Distinguished Service Order of the British military for this feat and left the service (after the war) a recognized hero. A 1957 British movie, *Ill Met by Moonlight*, is based on his exploits.

He was a genuine intellectual as well as a physically daring man, and he loved testing himself in fresh adventures. Because of his early training in the classics at King's School in Canterbury, England (from which he was expelled for holding hands with a girl), he developed an interest in writing. He decided that the best option for his skills and interests was to become a travel writer. This would allow him to explore unusual and little-known places. His books, *A Time of Gifts* and *Between the Woods and the Water* (based on a three-year walk across Europe in the 1930s) became international best sellers and, according to the New York Times, confirmed him as "the finest travel writer alive." Historian Robert Kaplan writes that his travel writing was special because he and other prominent travel writers of the same era had an "absence of electronic distractions [that] gave these writers time to read and hone their intellects, allowing them to describe cultures and landscapes in exquisite … language."

Fermor was happily married to Joan Monsell, a professional photographer. They lived in the Greek Islands where he entertained famous and interesting people for over 50 years. Historian Max Hastings calls him, "perhaps the most brilliant conversationalist of his time." Joan died in 2003, and Patrick followed her in 2011 at the age of 96.

Richard Woodward of the *New York Times* says that Fermor always loved his life and continually seized adventure. Woodward gives one explanation for this man's amazing life: ZEST. He writes that Fermor did everything with zest and verve. His life bubbled like a carbonated beverage. Zest for life, adventure, service, and people animated everything.

God has placed you here at this moment for a purpose. Always remember that your pursuit of that purpose is always done better with a little zest. Whatever God has called you to do, do it with joy and zest.

The Bible says in Nehemiah 8:10, *"The joy of the Lord is your strength." (NIV)*

Let the zest begin.

52 - Sensory Experience

Most scholars think they originated 3,000 years ago in Egypt, although some historians believe they started in China, around 200 B.C. Whatever the origin, all researchers agree that the ancient Romans perfected the technology.

They were the primary source of light for centuries. Their name comes from the Latin word *candla*, which is from the root word *candre*, meaning "to shine." They were made from animal products, such as beeswax or animal fat, until a group of American scientists discovered a use for a petroleum by-product in the 1850s. These researchers developed a substance they called paraffin, which quickly replaced the animal sources. Paraffin worked well but had a low melting point. The problem was solved by the addition of stearic acid. This combination created the modern candles. Scents were added in the 1990s, and marketers soon realized that the combination of warm lights and appealing fragrances created one of the most popular decorative items in the world. Modern candle development had stumbled on what many scientists had already learned: People were powerfully affected by sensory experience.

Dr. Harold Bloomfield writes, "According to researchers, the full development—and continued energetic use—of your senses may help promote lifelong physical, emotional and mental well-being. In response to heightened sensory activity, the nerve cells in the brain's cortex apparently grow larger and become more resistant to certain aging processes."

Dr. Robert Ornstein and Dr. David Sobel, writing in *Mental Medicine Update*, say that "in studies of workers with desk jobs, [access to] natural scenes nearly doubled satisfaction ratings. Workers with a view of nature felt less frustrated and more patient, found their jobs more challenging and interesting, expressed greater enthusiasm for their work, and reported greater overall satisfaction and health."

In addition, researchers at the University of Cincinnati found that fragrances in a room (such as found in candles) help people stay alert and improve performance.

God gave you your senses to experience the world. We now know that the use of those senses can enhance you as you interact with that world.

Let me suggest:

1. Experiment with different candle fragrances until you find what makes you feel happiest and most alert. One of my favorites is the Yankee Candle Company's "Mackintosh Apple." Find what works for you.
2. Put scenes of natural beauty where you can see them while you work.
3. Stop to look outside several times a day. If you can, go for short walks outdoors. Absorb nature through your senses to refresh your mind and emotions.

The Bible says in Genesis 2:8-9, "Now the LORD God had planted a garden in the east, in Eden; and there he put the man he had formed. The LORD God made all kinds of trees grow out of the ground—trees that were pleasing to the eye and good for food." (NIV)

Use your senses; they are a gift.

53 - Ear Power

What has the combined weight of a pick-up truck, an SUV, a van, and a compact car? If you guessed a 14,000 pound African bull elephant, then you are correct.

The elephant (both versions: African and Asian) is the largest land animal in the world. Its brain alone weighs 12 pounds, is highly developed, and sits at the back of the huge head for protection when the animal rams an object.

The elephant's trunk, an extension of its upper lip, has over 10,000 muscles, weighs 300 pounds, and is used for a wide variety of tasks. It can project sound (the famous trumpet call), detect numerous scents, work as a shovel, and pull in water to be deposited in the elephant's mouth or sprayed onto the animal like a shower. It is also used to carry objects, pick up food, and knock down heavy trees. I once watched an elephant in the wilds of South Africa pummel its way through a stand of trees by ramming and grabbing trees with its trunk. It was unstoppable.

Elephants have the largest ears of any animal. They are used to fan the elephant as a cooling mechanism and are very sensitive to sounds. They can detect even low frequency signals beneath what humans can receive. These ears are often a first line of defense.

Your human ears are also valuable. Dr. Alfred Tomatis wrote, "The primary importance of your hearing is to charge your nervous system." His 50-year research project on the importance of hearing also found that what you listen to is a powerful influence, "for problems related to energy level (tension and fatigue), loss of enthusiasm and depression."

Dr. Robert Cooper says that the music you listen to is especially effective in molding your emotional state and physical health.

He writes, "Music ... influences respiratory rate, blood pressure, stomach contractions and the level of stress hormones in your blood, and research suggests that it may also help strengthen your immune response."

You should listen to music that comforts, lifts, and inspires you. Composer George Rochberg even said that music "is closely related to the alpha logic of the central nervous system.... We listen with our whole bodies."

Let me suggest:

1. Take time every day to listen to music that elevates your spirit.
2. Start your day with music that makes you feel great.
3. Vary the music. Dr. Cooper says that, "some scientists believe that after 20 minutes or so, the nervous system may become over-sensitized to a specific tune and react with symptoms of distress."

The Bible says, *"Whenever the spirit from God came on Saul, David would take up his lyre and play. Then relief would come to Saul; he would feel better." (1 Samuel 16:23 NIV)*

54 - Open to the Unexpected

In March 1949, Jack Wrum, who was unemployed at the time, was walking off his frustration on a beach near San Francisco when he saw a bottle that had washed up on the sand. Curious, he opened the bottle, and his entire life changed.

In 1937, Daisy Singer Alexander was in London. She was an eccentric individual who sometimes did unexpected things. On one particular day, she decided to rewrite her will. When she finished, she stuffed the document in a bottle, jammed in a stopper, and tossed it into the River Thames. (This was the bottle Jack found 12 years later.)

When Jack opened the bottle and read the contents, he realized that he had located the last will and testament of an unknown woman. When he attempted to authenticate the document, he found that it belonged to an heir of the Singer Sewing Machine Company and was entirely legal. The will read, "To avoid any confusion, I leave my entire estate to the lucky person who finds this bottle, and to my attorney, Barry Cohen, share and share alike." It was signed Daisy Alexander and dated June 20, 1937.

Daisy had since died, so the will was in full effect. Jack received $6 million (in 1949 value) immediately and thereafter an annual income of $80,000. He was forever thankful he stopped to pick up the bottle.

Are you alert to the unexpected? Sometimes, something unplanned arrives that is exactly what you need. You just need to be watching. I was in an empty college cafeteria on a Saturday when I saw a young woman who captivated me. That young woman turned out to be God's choice for the person who would complete my life. Amy was unplanned and unexpected but has been the joy of my heart.

Let me suggest:

1. Sharpen your observation skills. Pay attention to little things.
2. Record your observations in a notebook or on an electronic device.
3. Be open to interruptions. They may contain the hidden message you are looking for.

The Bible says in Ecclesiastes 3:1, *"There is a time for everything, and a season for every activity under the heavens." (NIV)*

55 - Posture

It was believed to live in swamps near Lake Lerna in ancient Greece. For two thousand years local residents were convinced of its existence.

People who claimed to have seen it said it had a heavy body, which was covered with scales, and possessed a long reptilian tail that curved into a point. Some people said it had two feet; others said it had four. But all agreed that, whatever the number, the feet had sharp, dangerous claws. Some "witnesses" said it was the size of a baby elephant, while others swore it was as large as a dragon. Near-victims, those who had escaped the beast, claimed it had long, deadly teeth and breath that was noxious. Whatever the variety of description, everyone agreed that the most shocking feature of the creature was that it had multiple long necks, each topped by a vicious lunging head. The ancients called it the Hydra. Only the legendary Hercules was able to defeat it in direct combat.

The stories of the Hydra are so common that some scientists speculate it was an unknown species of dinosaur that survived into the time of man, although no fossils have been found that even remotely resemble such an animal. The Hydra remains a mystery.

Whatever you believe about the Hydra, the descriptions indicate that the beast had to carefully maintain its upright posture to support the weight of its writhing necks and large heads with snapping mouths. If it ever failed in holding its posture, it could lose control of its body and fall.

Your posture is also important. According to Dr. Harold Bloomfield, "poor posture distorts the alignment of bones and chronically tenses the muscles, and researchers report that it also contributes to conditions such as loss of lung capacity (as much as 30% or more); increased fatigue; reduced blood and oxygen to the brain and senses; limited range of motion, stiffness of joints and pain syndromes ... reduced mental alertness, reaction speed ... premature aging of body tissues; faulty digestion and constipation; back pain (perhaps 80% of all cases); and a tendency toward cynicism, pessimism, drowsiness and poor concentration." WOW! No wonder your mother always told you to sit up straight.

Here are some simple pointers:

1. Do not slump. According to Thomas Hanna, PhD, slumping is not inevitable and is "both avoidable and reversible." Slumping is a habit; not slumping is also a habit.
2. Take a moment before you sit to determine the most comfortable and balanced position. Remember that you can use an armrest to relieve around 25 percent of your weight.
3. Elevate the book or tablet up to your eye level to avoid bending your neck and dropping your head when you read.
4. Take a moment, several times a day, to "de-tense" your whole body and purposefully relax.

The Bible says in Psalm 40:2, *"He lifted me out of the slimy pit, out of the mud and mire; he set my feet on a rock."(NIV)*

Although this has a primarily spiritual application, it is also good advice for posture.

56 - Stand Up

In 1832, he was traveling on the paddle boat "Orleans", down the Mississippi River.

While walking on deck, he saw a distraught young man about to throw himself overboard and quickly moved to stop him. The young man was in despair. He was on the steamship with his new wife and had experienced a disaster. He had been entrusted with $60,000 (an enormous sum at that time) by a group of farmers. The money was intended for an investment in their collective businesses. The foolish young bridegroom had been invited to a card game, organized by three notorious gamblers, and had lost all the money. The man who rescued him asked to meet the bride and told the couple not to worry; everything would be all right.

The man located the ongoing card game and asked to join. He watched carefully as the professional gamblers operated. Soon, he observed the main gambler use a trick to win the round. He immediately stood, exposed the cheat, and demanded he surrender the money. The main gambler rose, full of anger and indignation, and challenged the stranger to a duel. Witnesses said the stranger smiled as he accepted the challenge. The offended gambler asked the stranger's name, and when he replied, the other two gamblers turned pale and begged their friend to apologize and leave. The offended gambler refused and climbed to the upper deck for the contest. He chose pistols (actually, derringers) and waited for the signal. By this time, a large crowd had gathered, and everyone was in suspense over the outcome.

The dishonest gambler suddenly fired first, but those watching said the stranger fired so fast that the gambler was dead before he hit the water. The stranger collected the stolen money and returned it to the amazed and grateful couple. He later said their persistent expressions of gratitude were so exuberant that he became embarrassed and debarked at the next stop.

The stranger who so gallantly saved the newlywed couple was Jim Bowie. He is still famous for the invention of the deadly frontier knife that bears his name, the bowie knife. Bowie eventually became known throughout the western territories as the "robin hood of the western wilds" for his good deeds and honorable actions. The knife became famous as the "American Short Sword." It was made by an Arkansas blacksmith, John Smith, using a secret process (still unknown today) that made it unbreakable, unbendable, and razor sharp. Bowie was carrying the knife when he dueled with the gambler. No doubt he would have used the knife if the pistol had failed (it had been done before).

The point of this is that Jim Bowie intervened when the young couple was in need. They were the victims of a cheating charlatan, and Bowie decided to do something about it. He decided to stand up and make a wrong into a right.

Sometimes you need to stand up and openly fight for what is right. The courage of one person can turn the tide.

Pick your battles carefully. Don't fight just because you disagree. Fight when you can make the difference for someone who needs your support and protection. Fight for godly principles and biblical morality. Sometimes people need a hero.

The Bible says, "'They will fight against you but will not overcome you, for I am with you and will rescue you,' declares the LORD." (Jeremiah 1:19 NIV)

57 - Get Over It

In 1979, the American Institute of Architects held their annual convention in Kansas City, Missouri. They had selected Kansas City so everyone could visit the building that had won their design award as "one of the finest buildings in the nation." The building, known as Kemper Arena, cost $12 million and was already famous for its wide spanning roof, which was considered a design of genius and inspiration. The journal *Architectural Record* said it had "an almost awesome masculinity." On the first day of the conference, architects swarmed through the building to see the national prize-winner for themselves. While they continued to view the structure on the second day, the roof suddenly collapsed. Twenty-six architects were hospitalized.

The same year in Grand Rapids, Michigan, the Allied Roofing and Siding Company was busy cleaning snow from roofs throughout the city when they were notified that their own roof had collapsed under the weight of snow.

In 1978, Ray Wright of Philadelphia was promoting his burglar alarm business by placing advertisements on the windshields of cars in a parking lot. The flyers read, "If you didn't see me put this on your windshield, I could have just as easily stolen your car." While Wright was passing out his information, someone stole his car.

In Jacksonville, Florida, the Riverside Chevrolet Company used a sales campaign with the slogan, "Look for it! Something BIG is going to happen!" A few hours after the launch of the campaign, the ceiling collapsed in their showroom, crushing six new cars.

In 1994, James Herriot, a British writer who had become famous for authoring *All Creatures Great and Small* (a book [it also inspired a television series] about the gentle ways of a country veterinarian), was hospitalized after he was attacked by a flock of sheep.

The lesson here is simple: Mistakes happen to everybody. Dumb things occur; this is a normal part of life. Don't stress over your mistakes and unexpected situations. Get over it! Life will go on.

Take a moment to write down two experiences when something happened that you thought was a disaster at the time. Write down what your life is like now. Did you survive?

The Bible says in Philippians 4:6–7, *"Do not be anxious about anything, but in every situation, by prayer and petition, with thanksgiving, present your requests to God. And the peace of God, which transcends all understanding, will guard your hearts and your minds in Christ Jesus." (NIV)*

Relax.

58 - Be Patient

In 1990, Doug and Brenda Cole went to an auction in Nashville, Tennessee. One of the items was the contents of an abandoned storage locker. According to the rules, they had to bid with no knowledge of what, if anything, it contained. They won with a bid of $50.

The locker had been abandoned by a recording engineer, and among the items were several boxes filled with tapes that had been recorded between 1953 and 1971. The couple listened to a few of the recordings and thought them interesting enough to contact Columbia Records to see if they would consider buying them. Columbia said No.

In 1992, they decided to try to get whatever they could for the old demos and finally sold them to Clark Enslin, owner of a small New Jersey record label, for $6,000.

Enslin decided he had something special and contacted Sun Records, the parent company of Columbia. Sun Records said that it wanted the demos but accused Enslin of obtaining them illegally and sued him for control of the contents of all the boxes.

After a three-year court battle, the judge ruled that Sun was entitled to 30 percent of the tapes because they contained songs recorded by artists who were under contract to it at the time of the recordings. Enslin was awarded the remaining 70 percent.

What did the boxes contain that prompted such a legal war? In the containers were more than 20,000 previously unreleased recordings by Bob Dylan, Elvis Presley, Johnny Cash, Roy Orbison, Louie Armstrong, and Frank Sinatra. The market value of Enslin's 70 percent was $100 million. There is no record of Doug and Brenda's response.

Do you need to wait a bit longer for your desired result? Do you need to fight a little longer? Be patient. Your greatest victory may still be ahead.

Take a moment to write down one dream that you have worked for that has not yet come true. Answer three questions:

1. Is this a dream you still want?

2. Have you done your best to accomplish this dream?

3. Does your dream please God?

If you answered yes, then it may be time to refocus on your dream. It still may come true.

The Bible says in Jeremiah 29:11, *"'For I know the plans I have for you,' declares the LORD, 'plans to prosper you and not to harm you, plans to give you hope and a future.'" (NIV)*

59 - Tough Enough

Some experts argue that Gurkha warriors may be the best fighters in the world. The Gurkhas are Hindu soldiers from deep in the Himalayan Mountains of Nepal. They have served as special forces for the British Army since 1816 and have won 13 Victoria Crosses (Great Britain's highest military honor).These soldiers have served in every major British military conflict from India to Iraq. They carry large curved blades called Gurkha knives and have been so fierce in combat in Afghanistan that the Taliban are terrified of them.

One of the most famous of Gurkha warriors was Bhanbhagta Gurung. On March 15, 1945, Gurung led a 10-man rifle squad to the base of a strategic hill on a Japanese-held island in the Pacific region. As Gurung led his men forward, they were ambushed by a sniper in a tree. When Gurung saw two of his men fall, he became so angry that he stood in full view (with bullets whizzing all around him), drew a careful bead on the sniper and blew him out of the tree. Gurung then ran up the hill for twenty yards (as machine guns were trying to cut him down) and attacked a concrete fortification at the top. He tossed concussion grenades into the bunker, leaped inside, and killed everyone with a bayonet. He charged another shelter and killed those occupants as well.

At this point, he was pinned down by machine gun fire from another site. He promptly stood up, dodged every bullet, and ran straight at the gun emplacement. He dove into this bunker and realized that the interior was too tight to use his rifle, so he drew his Gurkha knife and killed everyone inside. By the time he was finished, the hilltop was in Gurkha hands and 66 Japanese soldiers were dead.

When the war ended, Gurung went home to his (according to

sources) very attractive wife, reared three sons, and cared for his ill mother. He died in 2008 at the age of 87.

Sometimes you have to be tough. When life knocks you down, you get back up and go again. You become an unstoppable force.

How do you do this? It starts in your mind. Studies at Harvard Medical School have found that resilience is a key to long life and good health. Another term for this is "mental toughness."

Your first thought when facing adversity is critical. Your first thought helps create your response. If you train yourself to immediately think, I'm OK. I can do this; God will help me (or other inspiring statements), you will bring up your courage and strengthen your determination. You can always ask God to give you strength and fortitude. You can be tough enough.

The Bible says that when David heard about the 9-foot-tall Goliath, he said to King Saul, *"Let no one lose heart on account of this [giant]; your servant will go and fight him. The LORD who delivered me from the paw of the lion and from the paw of the bear will deliver me from the hand of this Philistine." (1 Samuel 17:32 NIV, 1 Samuel 17:37 ESV)* And God did!

60 - Avoid the Poison

The king cobra is the largest poisonous snake in the world. The toxins released by it's bite are powerful enough to kill an adult elephant. Most full-grown king cobras are 14 feet long and the longest ever measured was 18 feet. When aroused it inflates it's hood and rises 5 to 6 feet straight up, in preparation to strike.

The taipan is a 10 foot long snake with enough venom to kill 10,000 mice. It is a native of Australia where locals call it the "fierce snake"—although it is actually very shy and avoids contact with humans. Someone bitten by a taipan will die in minutes.

The mamba is native to Africa and can be either green or black. It grows up to 14 feet but 10 feet is more common. It lives among rocks and tall grass and is the most feared snake in the entire African continent. The mamba is also the fastest snake in the world, reaching speeds of 15 miles per hour. It is also the only snake known to actively stalk humans. Two drops of black mamba venom can kill an adult human in 10 minutes. The green mambas are 5-7 feet long, live in trees and are almost as deadly as the black.

The largest deadly viper in the world is the bushmaster, found mostly in Central America. It is particularly dangerous because it attacks when confronted by a human rather than seeking escape, as do most snakes. It has one inch fangs and carries enough toxin to kill with enough left to keep killing.

Roger Caras, well-known expert on snakes (a herpetologist,) lists the 10 most deadly snakes in the world as:

1. King Cobra
2. Taipan
3. Mamba
4. Bushmaster
5. Western Diamondback Rattlesnake
6. Fer-De-Lance
7. Tropical Rattlesnake
8. Tiger Snake
9. Common Cobra
10. Jarracussa

You will probably never encounter one of these dangerous reptiles but you often come into contact with another venomous creature. Many of you have experienced the poison of a negative individual; a human "snake" who "bites" you with criticism and wounds you with hurtful words. Ann Sexton, writer and poetess, said that the one thing a person should never do is destroy another person. You should never send venom into the heart of someone else.

Oswald Chambers was a devout Christian and Bible teacher who was well-known as a man with a deep spiritual relationship with Jesus Christ. He had an unusual ability to explain profound principles. After he died in 1917, in Cairo, Egypt, while serving as a chaplain for the British military, his wife Gertrude began to compile excerpts from Chamber's many sermons and lectures. In 1924, she published them under the title, *My Utmost for His Highest*. This collection of daily devotional readings is now the best-selling devotional guide in history. In one of these readings, Chambers writes that God does not allow you to see the flaws of another person so you can attack or criticize them; He lets you see the flaws so you can love, help and pray for them. What great advice! Trade venom for love.

Do three things now.

1. Make a list of people you have animosity toward and forgive them.
2. Train yourself to only say positive comments about other people.
3. If you are in a dispute with someone then write down their name and pray daily for them and for your relationship.

Jesus said in John 13:35, *"By this shall all men know you are my disciples, if you love one another."*

61 - Invention

Mountain Dew was invented in the 1940's by Ally Hartman, of Knoxville, Tennessee. He intended it to be used as a chaser for Tennessee whisky. Mountain Dew originally looked and tasted like 7UP, but the formula was changed after Hartman sold it in 1954. In 1961, William Jones bought the product and decided to test several ideas related to taste. For three years, Jones experimented with different ingredients by adding various levels of citrus flavoring and caffeine. He then traveled to high schools and factories with the drinks in small cups labeled A, B, C, and D to ask people which contents they liked best. He used this information to balance his formula, which eventually became the Mountain Dew we have today. When Jones finished this process, he sold the formula to the Pepsi Company, who marketed and sold the drink.

In 1933, W.G. Peacock started the New England Products Company. The business specialized in spinach, lettuce, and other vegetable juices. The company advertised the drinks widely but failed to find a market; people just didn't like them. Peacock refused to admit defeat. He tried different vegetable combinations for a year until he arrived at a mixture he thought tasted good enough to sell. The product contained tomato, celery, carrot, spinach, lettuce, watercress, beet, and parsley juices. He called it Vege-min. Customers liked the combined flavors and sales grew steadily. Peacock designed a can label with a large V and a list of all eight ingredients. He gave a free sample to a grocer in Evanston, Illinois, and the grocer suggested a simple change—a giant V and the number 8. Peacock liked the idea, and V8 vegetable juice was on its way into the American diet.

Roy Allen had a successful business buying and selling hotel properties during Prohibition. One day, he met a man, who operated a soda fountain, who gave him his formula for root beer.

The man told Allen that, because of Prohibition, he could make a fortune selling 5-cent root beer. Allen decided to experiment, so he opened a root beer stand in Lodi, California, in 1919. He designed the stand to look like an Old West saloon with sawdust on the floor. The business was so successful he opened a second location in Stockton, California, with an employee, Frank Wright, as a partner. The beverage proved so popular that the two men devoted their time to the expansion of their root beer business. In 1922, they decided to give the company and the root beer a new name. They combined the first initial of each of their last names and called the venture A &W.

You never know where an idea could lead. Allow your creativity to flow. Follow your inventive thought to its destination and see what happens.

Let me suggest:

1. Write your creative idea down IMMEDIATELY. People lose ideas continually by not recording them. I know; it's happened to me too many times.
2. Research the rules of registering inventions and patents so you can be ready if an idea develops into something real.
3. Be patient and work your idea. Most good results come from experimentation and effort.
4. Remember, a useful idea does not have to be for something tangible. Maybe your best idea will be a new and better way to do something.
5. Have fun!

The Bible says in Ecclesiastes 10:10, *"If the ax is dull and its edge unsharpened, more strength is needed, but skill will bring success."* (NIV)

Keep your creative "ax" sharp and see what happens.

62 - The Phone Call

The first phone directory was published in 1878, two years after Alexander Graham Bell introduced the first working telephone. It was issued by the Telephone Dispatch Company of Boston. It was one page long because only 97 Bostonians had a phone. It also had no phone numbers because a method for dialing had not been invented yet. You made a call by picking up a receiver and turning a hand crank that rang a bell to signal an operator. When the operator answered, you told her (they were all women) who you wanted to call; and she completed the process.

The first business directories were printed on white paper by the Chicago printing firm of R.R. Donnelley and contained only addresses. If a business had a phone, the printing company simply noted that fact without listing a number. Bell Telephone issued its first business directory with actual phone numbers in 1878. It was one page long and had only seven business categories: Physicians, Dentists, Stores, Factories, Meat and Fish Markets, Miscellaneous, and Hack [horses for hire] and Boarding Stables.

Business directories were first printed on yellow paper in 1881. The Wyoming Telephone and Telegraph Company hired a printer in Cheyenne to do its directory; the printer did not have enough white paper to complete the order, so he used the only other color he had available: yellow. The (again) single-page directory had only 100 listings, with such local headings as Boots, American Indian Jewelry, and Soda Water Companies. When advertisers discovered the possibilities of the directories, they exploded in value and popularity.

All of this happened because people wanted to establish voice contact with other people. When was the last time you called another human being to just chat? I'm not talking an email or text, but an actual conversation? Most people only speak by phone to anonymous individuals in customer service when trying to resolve a problem. Phone contact may be becoming a lost art.

I suspect that people avoid phone connection because they are either in a hurry and consider an electronic form of communication quicker and more convenient (you can control the length of contact by the length of your message), or they do not want to speak directly with the other person because of a possible negative confrontation. In either case, they may miss an important opportunity for discussion.

Let me suggest:

1. Make a list of 10 people whose relationship you value. Take two days and call all ten. Let them know you are calling just because you wanted to refresh the relationship. Be sure you ask about their lives; let them do most of the talking.
2. Make a list of specific social skills that can better develop in actual conversations. Practice those skills in three conversations this week.

Even God responds to a call. The Bible says in Jeremiah 33:3, *"'Call to me and I will answer you and tell you great and unsearchable things you do not know.' For this is what the LORD, the God of Israel, says." (NIV)*

63 - Look at the Facts

Have you heard of Snowball the monster cat?

In early 2000 a picture of a bearded man holding a cat circulated on the Internet. There was nothing unusual about a man holding a cat, but this cat was huge, the size of a Labrador dog. To put it another way, the giant white cat was half the size of the large man holding it.

The media became interested, and the story of the monster cat was featured on NBC's The Tonight Show with Jay Leno and ABC's Good Morning America. The news stories fed the demand for more information, and several investigative reports began to pursue the story. The information uncovered revealed that the cat, named Snowball, was owned by Rodger Degagne of Ottawa, Canada. According to the reports, Rodger had found an abandoned cat wandering alone outside the grounds of a Canadian nuclear facility and had taken it home. This cat later gave birth to kittens, one of which was Snowball, who rapidly grew until she reached an astounding 87 pounds. Rodger and his family were so amazed that they took a picture of Rodger holding the enormous cat and posted it on the Internet. Soon the picture went viral; it caught the attention of American TV networks and was featured in several magazines and newspapers. The monster cat had become a sensational celebrity.

The only problem was that the whole story was a fake. In May 2001, Cordell Hauglie of Edmonds, Washington, admitted that the cat's actual name was Jumper, a pet owned by his daughter, and weighed a normal 21 pounds. He (Rodger Degagne of Canada did not exist) had used photo manipulation software to create the picture of him holding Jumper and then had emailed it to some friends "as a joke." He said he did not realize what had happened until he saw stories of "Snowball, the Monster Cat" on TV.

This is an example of the danger of not checking the facts. It is remarkable that even seasoned reporters and television executives were fooled by a story they apparently wanted to believe. Gullibility is epidemic in our culture. I saw an on-the-street series of recent TV interviews and heard a reporter ask a young woman (a college graduate) what she thought of Vice President Paul Ryan. She considered the question for a moment and said that she thought he was doing a fine job. It is scary to think that we have such a population of uninformed citizens. They are the type of people who can be easily manipulated.

Let me suggest:

1. Check the facts before you accept a story or claim you encounter in the media (TV, Internet, newspapers, and magazines).
2. Research the credibility of who you read or listen to. Don't believe someone just because he claims to be an expert or a celebrity.
3. Understand your own biases. Make sure you don't accept a story just because it says what you want to believe.

You can be a more effective leader by focusing on accuracy. You will stand out when you develop a reputation for knowing the facts.

The Bible says, *"Speak the truth to each other, and render true and sound judgment in your courts." (Zechariah 8:16 NIV)*

64 - Keep Trying

In the summer of 1904 the International Olympic Games were held in St. Louis, Missouri. It was the most bizarre Olympic competition in history.

The modern Olympics were reinvented in 1896, so this Olympics was only the third since the new beginning. The organizers were uncertain how to bring the games into the 20th century, so they decided to experiment with what nations to invite and what sports to include.

Their first major blunder was to move the games from Chicago to St. Louis, which was a bad decision because the St. Louis World's Fair was already scheduled for the same time. Because of this, the crowds were so low that financial disaster was inevitable. Even Pierre de Coubertin, the founder of the modern Olympics, refused to attend.

When the event began, the committee announced that certain dates during the competition were set aside as "anthropology days." On these dates, certain "primitive" tribes that "had been especially selected" participated in events that were supposed to be "appropriate" for their level of development.

One of the most memorable clashes was between the "Pygmies" and the "Patagonians." Spectators watched as members of the two tribes competed in mud-fighting, greased pole climbing, rock tossing, and spear throwing. The attendance was small.

The games were such a fiasco that the committee decided to hold the games only two years later in Athens, Greece (home of the original Olympics), to try to restore some dignity and attract more people. The 1904 Summer Olympics is still famous as one of the craziest ever.

The spectacular success and huge popularity of today's Olympic Games are proof of what can happen if you just keep trying. The Olympic organizers learned their lessons and moved forward.

Michael Jordan, the greatest basketball player of all time, lost his first SIX playoffs before winning his first championship. Babe Ruth struck out 1,360 times on the way to becoming the greatest baseball player, ever.

Don't lose your nerve; don't give in. Never stop trying.

Everybody remembers the ones who didn't quit.

Write your most important personal goal. Renew your commitment to that goal and write a list of ways to accomplish it.

The Bible says in Galatians 6:9, *"Let us not become weary in doing good, for at the proper time we will reap a harvest if we do not give up." (NIV)*

65 - Maximum Ingenuity

Roger Corman has always been different.

When he was 32, he had already been directing commercial films for five years. He had developed a reputation for low-budget, quickly produced horror films such as *Monster from the Ocean Floor* and *Attack of the Crab Monsters*. His skill with this type of entertainment eventually led him to be called "King of the B Films."

In 1959, Roger finished his newest movie *A Bucket of Blood* (he described it as a "beatnik-styled horror comedy") in only five days and bet a friend that he could do his next feature in 48 hours.

Because of the tight budget (almost non-existent), he asked his scriptwriter Chuck Griffith to take the script for *A Bucket of Blood* and redo it for the next film. He stipulated that whatever Griffith wrote would have to fit with the existing set because there was no money for a new one. A week later, after the new script was finished, Corman hired an unknown 23-year-old actor named Jack Nicholson, rehearsed the movie for three days, and shot the footage in two days. His total cost was $30,000, and he called the final production *The Passionate People Eater*. The musical score was a reworked version of the music that had been used for *A Bucket of Blood*, a score that had already been used for *The Wasp Woman* and would be used again for *Creature from the Haunted Sea*. Roger paid $317.34 for the music. For a skid row scene with bums, Corman actually filmed in Skid Row. In order to save money, he paid street people 10 cents per scene. When he needed one more actor, he drafted Griffith, the scriptwriter, to play three different characters.

To this day, the film holds the record for the shortest filming time of any movie. It is in the Guinness World Records as having "the shortest shooting schedule for a full-length, commercial feature film made without stock footage."

The film, under its new name, *The Little Shop of Horrors*, was a moderate success but became a cult classic on late-night television. It was introduced off Broadway in 1982 and made into a $20 million film in 1987. It has since become a successful Broadway production that continues to be performed.

What ideas have you abandoned because you think you don't have the money or resources to make them happen? Roger Corman believed in his vision so much that he used maximum ingenuity to bring it to fulfillment. He did not focus on the difficulties; he looked at the possibilities. He used what he had to create what he needed.

Try this:

1. Write down two ideas that fill you with excitement. Next to each idea write the words, "Can I do this?" Go back and add the word "how" to the beginning of the sentence so it reads, "How can I do this?" Answer that question.
2. Take both ideas and decide on what first step you would need to take to test them.
3. Take the first steps.

The Bible says in Proverbs 13:12, *"Hope deferred makes the heart sick, but a longing fulfilled is a tree of life." (NIV)*

Don't wait for perfect conditions. See what you can do with maximum ingenuity.

66 - Think First

In 1974, the Consumer Product Safety Commission ordered 80,000 buttons for a national campaign to warn parents about the possible dangers of children's toys. The buttons were printed with the words, "For Kids' Sake, Think Toy Safety." The government agency quickly recalled all 80,000 buttons when it discovered serious safety issues. The agency released a statement that said the buttons put children at risk because they had, "sharp edges, parts a child could swallow, and were coated with toxic lead paint." OOPS!

The town council of Winchester, Indiana, once passed a statute prohibiting the sale of pornography within the city limits. When the local newspaper received a copy of the new law, the editors saw that it was full of such graphic pornographic examples that they refused to print the document. Because another local ordinance specified that no statute could become law unless first published in the local newspaper, the anti-pornography legislation never became law, and porn continued to be available to anyone who wanted to buy it.

The San Diego County Sheriff's Department decided to teach the community the hazards of the private use of fireworks. A group of deputies and firefighters met at a bomb disposal facility outside the city and detonated thousands of illegal fireworks. Local news media recorded the disaster as sparks flew out of the building, igniting a 10-acre brush fire that took 50 firefighters, two water-dispensing helicopters, and a bulldozer to extinguish.

On December 31, 1903, the Iroquois Theater in Chicago opened with wide publicity as the "world's first fireproof theater." One month later, it burned to the ground.

On the evening of September 20, 1996, author Bertil Torekull gave a lecture to 300 people in the Stifts-och Landsbibliotek library in Stockholm, Sweden. Just after he finished his presentation on book burning, the fire alarm sounded. Everyone was evacuated, but the library was completely destroyed by fire.

The next time you make a plan, make sure you think first. Examine the possible consequences of what you are doing. Try to anticipate different results of what you are pursuing. The extra time you take to think through each part of your plan could protect you from unintended consequences.

Stop and write a brief description of something you are currently planning. Break the plan into small understandable segments. Write what could go wrong with each segment. Make a new plan that deals with those possibilities. Think of ways to secure your success.

The Bible says in Proverbs 20:25, *"It is a trap to dedicate something rashly and only later to consider one's vows." (NIV)*

THINK!

67 - Be Aggressive

He was from a wealthy California family and his grandfather had been the mayor of Los Angeles.

When he was 26, he competed in the Summer Olympics in Stockholm, Sweden, in marksmanship with a pistol. He missed getting a gold medal because of a technicality. He developed an interest in swords and eventually became one of the top-rated fencers in the United States.

He struggled in school and did so poorly in mathematics that he had to repeat his first year of college. He finally graduated number 43 out of a class of 103.

He served in the United States Army in World War I and was badly wounded while leading a charge against a machine gun nest. He continued to fight and lead his men for over an hour, despite his injuries. When he reached high rank in World War II, his commanding officer at first refused to appoint him head of a major assault because he thought him "too undisciplined."

He was an emotional man who once left a stage in tears when he was asked to address soldiers (men he had commanded earlier) at Fort Bragg, North Carolina. He was overcome when he looked at the men who would soon fight and die and could not speak because of his great love and affection for them. When he realized that he would have to inspire men by public speaking, he devoted months to practicing in front of a mirror so he could better motivate his men.

When he finally achieved command of an army group, he addressed the troops and told them, "If you don't succeed, I don't want to see you alive. I see no point in surviving defeat, and I'm sure that if all of you enter into battle with equal resolution, we shall conquer, and live long, and gain more glory." As for the German enemy soldiers, his men should "grab those pusillanimous SOB's by the nose and kick 'em in the @#%!@'s and slaughter the lousy Hun @@#$%#@%s by the bushel."

President Franklin Roosevelt wrote in his diary, following his first meeting with the general, that he was "a joy." Roosevelt later stated that in this man he had found a man who would fight. One historian summed up the general's philosophy of war as simply hitting the enemy "everywhere with everything."

It is no surprise that the German High Command feared George Patton more than any other foe.

Sometimes you need to be aggressive. Sometimes you have to push yourself to win. Sometimes you have to throw caution out and seize your opportunity.

Make a list of the dominant fears that hold you back. Be specific. Next, write a paragraph on each fear, explaining why it stops you. Take each fear and make a plan to conquer it. Get started. Be aggressive.

God says in Joshua 1:9, *"I have commanded you, 'Be strong and courageous! Don't tremble or be terrified, because the LORD your God is with you wherever you go.'"(GW)*

If God is leading you to do something, don't wait. Be aggressive in your response.

68 - Needless Enemies

James Gallo and Joe Conigliaro decided to murder Vinny Ensulo because Vinny had slipped information about their crime group to the police. He was, according to the gang, a "stool pigeon."

On November 1, 1973, Gallo and Conigliaro grabbed Vinny off Columbia Street in Brooklyn, New York, and shoved him into a car. Witnesses say shots were heard and the car swerved violently then stopped. The two gangsters had placed Vinny between them and fired, missing Vinny but hitting each other. Conigliaro survived but was struck in the spine and paralyzed. Vinny, who got away, sent wheelchair batteries to Joe on each anniversary of the shooting with a card that read, "Keep rolling, from your best pal, Vinny...."

The June 5, 1995 edition of Forbes Magazine reported a story of a California attorney, Theresa McConville, who sold a vacant lot she owned in Ventura County. She took bids for the property, including one from a local anesthesiologist, Reynaldo Fong. When Fong lost the bid, he was so enraged he vowed revenge. For the next ten years, he took out almost 10,000 magazine subscriptions in McConville's name, giving her address for billing. He also once arranged for a refrigerator to be delivered to the attorney, COD (cash on delivery). It cost McConville thousands of dollars to straighten out the mess.

A strange incident took place near Louisville, Kentucky. A group of men was returning from a hunting trip when one of them saw the paw of a rabbit reach from a bag carried by one of their companions, grab the handle of the shotgun in his hand, pull the trigger, and shoot the man in the foot.

A good friend once told me never to make a needless enemy.

You never know what that person might do in retaliation. Always calculate the possible results when you face a conflict with someone else. Simply put, is the conflict worth the potential trouble?

The Bible says that, *"God has called us to live in peace." (1 Corinthians 7:17 NIV)* And Jesus said to *"love your enemies and pray for those who persecute you." (Matthew 5:44 NIV)*

Always watch out for the boomerang effect when you are tempted to seek revenge: The poison you spray toward someone else will splash back on you.

1. Make a list of people who have wronged you.
2. Pray for each one.
3. Release your bitterness and forgive them.
4. Enjoy the freedom you sense as you let go of your enemies.

The Bible says in Colossians 3:13, *"Bear with each other and forgive one another if any of you has a grievance against someone. Forgive as the Lord forgave you." (NIV)*

You don't need more enemies; you need more friends.

69 - Don't Stop Believing

You have never heard a story like this from me. The usual introduction to my contact with you is an unusual story uncovered in my research. Today is different, very different. I am going to open a private window and give you a glimpse into my life. I am taking this action because I believe someone needs this message today.

Three times, I have been at the end of all my opportunities. Three times, I have been on the edge of disaster when all hope seemed gone, and three times an unexpected shift saved me. The first time happened when Amy and I had returned from a series of speaking engagements. We arrived at our apartment in Lexington, Kentucky, late and tired. Our small non-profit company was less than two years old, and we were working overtime to build our dream of positive, Christian-based success seminars. I dropped our bags in the hallway and picked up two weeks of accumulated mail. I carried the mail into the front room and began to sort through each item. I stopped when an envelope with three capital letters caught my attention. As I opened the flap, I wondered why the IRS had sent me a letter. It was the worst news I could have imagined. I was being notified that the agency had not received our quarterly employee payments for almost a year and was demanding full and immediate payment, plus penalties and interest. I was told I would be facing serious legal action, which might include a felony charge. I was shocked and uncertain. I had delegated all financial affairs to a friend who had volunteered to handle all our accounts. When I called him, he didn't answer. My first reaction was to tell Amy what had happened and then pray. I felt numb and empty inside. I asked God to help and guide us, and we went to bed.

The next morning, I discovered that all our accounts had been drained of money. We were broke and overdrawn. I was still unable to reach my friend who managed our business; he had disappeared. Throughout the day, I wavered between faith and despair. At one point, I sat on a bottom stair step and held my head in my hands, unable to move. When the panic passed, Amy and I prayed again and asked God for a miracle. That was on a Monday.

On Tuesday morning, I woke early and went into the kitchen to read, pray, and put myself at God's disposal. I told Him that He was my only hope, and I would trust Him to rescue me. At 10 a.m. I was suddenly aware of a voice in my mind that said, "Call Phyllis Ranier." I was puzzled. Phyllis was a family friend who lived in my home town. I had not seen her for several years and did not even know her well. At 11 a.m. I called her home number. She answered and asked me why I had called. My emotional control collapsed, and I poured my story into the phone receiver. She listened then asked me how much money I needed. I gave the exact figure, including the 32 cents that came at the end. Phyllis said everything would be all right because she had my money. I asked her to explain. She replied that she kept a special account, which she used to give gifts to Christian ministries. The amount in that account was precisely the same as the amount I needed, even down to the 32 cents. She had planned on sending the money to a particular organization but had sensed God telling her to wait. He told her that the person for whom the money was meant would call for it on Tuesday morning. God had given us an amazing miracle. We were so thankful at how He had engineered the perfect answer at the perfect moment.

Have you ever been at a dark and difficult moment when your resources were inadequate to help you? Are you at such a place now? Why don't you ask God to give you the answer you need? Don't stop believing. The Bible says, *"For I am the LORD your God who takes hold of your right hand and says to you, Do not fear; I will help you." (Isaiah 41:13 NIV)*

70 - The Generosity Surprise

On December 14, 1996, the employees of Kingston Technology Company, Inc. received an unexpected Christmas bonus. The amounts varied, but the median gift was $130,000 ($190,000 in today's money).

The company founders and owners, John Tu and David Sun, both immigrants from Taiwan, had always cared for their workers. In 1995, when Kingston passed $1 billion in annual revenue, the two men bought ads in newspapers across America that said "Thanks a billion" and listed each employee by name.

In August 1996, they sold 80 percent of Kingston to Softbank for $1.5 billion. No one would have questioned the two if they had retired with their profits, but they decided to surprise their former employees by giving them $100 million to be distributed as Christmas bonuses.

The generosity of Tu and Sun is an inspiration, but there is an even more meaningful end to their story. Three years after the sale, they had an opportunity to repurchase their company for only $450 million. They now had the immense profits from the original sale and ownership of the company again.

From 1999 to 2012, the company grew to 4,000 employees. The two founders have continued their generous and compassionate leadership, and everyone has prospered together. In 2011, Forbes Magazine listed Kingston as the second-largest privately owned tech-hardware company in the United States and one of the best places to work in the United States, which is not surprising considering the beneficent commitment of its owners. When Tu and Sun gave their unexpected and extraordinary gift to their employees in 1996, it started a chain reaction of rewards. Within three years, their investment in giving had brought big dividends.

This is God's law of giving and receiving. God always blesses generosity; He always rewards giving. This is a law that God has built into His universe.

Several years ago, Amy and I had a financial crisis. In July of that year, we had $3,000 in the bank and no way to pay multiple bills. I was watching an online church when God moved my heart to give that ministry $1,000. Amy agreed, and we transferred the money. Into the next month, the crisis worsened. By mid-August we were broke. We decided to trust God and believe that He would reward our gift. The next week, money poured in until we had received $30,000. God proved Himself faithful. We have never forgotten that lesson.

I once encountered an investment counselor from Philadelphia. He was a non-practicing Jew who claimed to be an atheist. He said that he always counseled every client to select a church or charity and give to it. He said that, over the years, he had observed that those who gave always received more. He admitted that he did not understand why, but the results were obvious and consistent.

Be generous. You may be surprised at the results.

Jesus said in Luke 6:38, *"Give, and it will be given to you. A good measure, pressed down, shaken together and running over, will be poured into your lap. For with the measure you use, it will be measured to you." (NIV)*

71 - The Challenge of Change

On March 29, 1848, a local farmer became restless and decided to take a walk. He left his house a little before midnight and followed a well-known path. After he had strolled a short distance, he suddenly heard something disturbing: silence.

The farmer hurried home and alerted friends and family that the unthinkable had happened: The mighty Niagara Falls had stopped. There was no ferocious roar of cascading water, no torrents of liquid; there was nothing. The falls were virtually dry.

The next morning, people who always awoke to the deafening sound of the falls, now awoke to silence. They gathered in groups along the edge of the gorge to see the unexpected sight of a river that had (overnight) become a trickle. Local citizens climbed to the empty riverbed amidst hundreds of dead fish and floundering turtles. People walked the surface collecting souvenirs of guns, bayonets, and American Indian tomahawks that had been exposed by the absence of the water.

When word spread of the situation, thousands filled churches to pray. Panic began to spread, and some feared the end of the world. Throughout that day and the next, anxious people sought any news that would explain the phenomenon. Soon the explanation arrived.

Word came from nearby Buffalo, New York, that a huge storm had pushed giant blocks of ice to the northeastern edge of Lake Erie, where they had jammed the inlet into the Niagara River. This monstrous ice dam had stopped the river and as a result, the Niagara Falls.

While people waited for the ice to move, crowds explored the riverbed, and the owner of the tour boat, The Maid of the

Mist, used explosives to remove several boulders that had always caused the boat difficulty.

No water flowed for 40 hours (from March 30 to the early morning hours of March 31). Then a faint rumble was heard by those still gathered at the site, and soon an enormous wall of foaming water came pouring into the gorge restoring the falls. The ice dam had broken, and all was back to normal.

How do you handle change? Change is an absolute certainty in life. You may think that everything will always stay the same, but change will happen anyway. So again, how do you handle change? How do you prepare for the unexpected?

Let me suggest:

1. Accept the facts. Don't waste time and emotion resisting reality.
2. Have an adventurous attitude. Draw the positive from change and make it work for you. Have fun with the changes. Recognize that change can be good.
3. Do your best to prepare for different possibilities, then don't worry; don't stress over what you can't control.
4. Trust God; He can handle anything. He knows what's coming, and He loves you. You can depend on Him.

Remember the Bible says in Malachi 3:6, *"I the LORD do not change." (NIV)*

72 - Improvement

George Beauchamp and Adolph Rickenbacker were first.

Their invention amplified sound from a device they called "lap steel." Their purpose was to enable the item to produce a sound that could not be overpowered by sounds from other devices in the area. They used magnets wrapped in slender coils of wire, and they designed the invention so a person could hold it in his lap to create sound by sliding a metal bar up and down the magnetized wires.

Guy Hart saw a demonstration of one of the devices and decided that it could be dramatically improved. He asked engineers in his company to use the basic magnet idea and develop something more usable that the company could then sell. The engineering team designed a flat steel blade that was placed vertically under the wires. They then positioned two heavy magnets beneath the assembly and coiled the wire around the blade on top of the magnets.

The new design produced superior sound but still needed a package that would appeal to the public. So the engineers designed a shell around the sound box. (They used one of the most brilliant insights in the history of marketing when they decided to target a buying group of young men.) They chose to make the casing like the contours of a young woman's body—rounded curves, shoulders, and a scooped waist. They added an electric amplifier and proceeded to make music history.

The company patented its product as the only musical instrument that had to be plugged in (to the amplifier) to make sounds. The company called its instrument the E-150 and started selling it (in 1935) with the amplifier for $150 (around $2,500 today).

The Gibson Company's electric guitar changed the entertainment world forever—all because one man decided to improve someone else's idea.

Remember this: You don't have to have the best (or even the first) idea to create success. Sometimes you just need to improve on what's already there.

Do this:

1. Make a list of two things that could make your life better if you simply improved them.
2. Improve them both and keep making lists until you have improved the entire structure of your life.
3. Have fun!

The Bible says that "the plans of the diligent lead to profit." (Proverbs 21:5 NIV)

73 - Expect a Miracle

In 1967, a music group called the Youngbloods released their first record on the RCA label, "Grizzly Bear." It was moderately successful, but their follow-up recording was a dismal flop. It climbed to #62 on the *Billboard* chart then faded into oblivion. The song was a call for people everywhere to love one another and "get along."

Two years later, the National Conference of Christians and Jews launched a campaign called National Brotherhood Week. The group organized programming across numerous media outlets, including television. The programming packets were sent to TV and radio stations across America and included a recording of the failed song by the Youngbloods (without their knowledge).

The campaign received little response, but the obscure song became a sensation. Radio stations were flooded with requests for the number. Soon the song became a huge hit, climbing into the top ten and selling 2 million copies. The recording was titled *Get Together*, and the refrain is still recognized today: "Come on people, smile on your brother/ Everybody get together, try to love one another right now."

Another musical miracle took place in 1967 when Edwin Hawkins started the 46-member Northern California State Youth Choir. He needed to raise money for the choir to continue, so he selected eight singers and recorded an album in the basement of a local church. They were happy to sell 600 copies.

That same year, a music promoter in San Francisco found a copy of the album in a warehouse and gave it to a popular local DJ, Abe "Voco" Kesh, who loved it and played it enough to make it a local hit. Other stations then picked up on one of the songs and began to expand its airtime. Suddenly, the recording jumped all boundaries and went viral. Over a million copies were sold. People could not get enough of *Oh Happy Day*.

Learn to trust God and expect miracles. God's timing may not be your timing, but He always fulfills His purposes and His promises. Believe that each day could be the great day that delivers the miracle that could change your life.

The Bible says in Psalms 5:3, *"In the morning, LORD, you hear my voice; in the morning I lay my requests before you and wait expectantly." (NIV)*

Expect a miracle today.

74 - It's Not Over Yet

The following are actual movie reviews, written by popular and respected film critics.

"I regret to report that it is just another movie, so thoroughly mixed with water as to have a horror content of about .0001 percent.... The film ... soon turns into sort of a comic opera with a range of cardboard mountains over which extras in French Revolution costumes dash about with flaming torches."
—*Outlook & Review Magazine*

"The [film] is a genuinely funny comedy which succeeds despite an uninteresting and untalented actor in the title role."
—*Films in Review*

"As a thriller, it lacks logic. As a cop film, it throws standard police procedures, and with them, any hope of authenticity, to the wind. As a showcase for the martial arts, it's a disappointment ... and as action-adventure, it's pointlessly puerile." — *Chicago Tribune*

"An overly grandiose script, performed with relentless grandiloquence.... Up to a point I'm willing to overlook the egg on a guy's face, but, really, there's such a thing as too much—especially when they're promoting this bloated, pseudo-epic as a low-budget Oscar-bound winner." —*Washington Star*

"[The director] seems to have been more interested in shocking his audience ... and in photographing [his lead actress] in various stages of undress, than in observing the ordinary rules for good film construction. This is a dangerous corner for a gifted moviemaker to place himself in." —*America Magazine*

The reviews were comments on the following (in order): *Frankenstein*, Dustin Hoffman in *The Graduate*, *Lethal Weapon*,

Rocky, and Alfred Hitchcock's *Psycho.* Obviously, these critics were wrong.

You can learn important lessons from this journey into the world of film reviews.

1. You don't have to absorb the negative review of you or of your performance. Your worst critic can still be wrong, and you may actually be right.
2. You must always learn from your critics. Be smart enough to use a critical comment to create improvement. (There may be some valid points in the criticism that you can use to your benefit.)
3. You must try not to make the critic an enemy. Show grace and forgiveness.
4. You can ask God to give you guidance—then listen when He answers. He is not your critic; He is your loving Father.

The Bible says in James 1:5, *"If any of you lacks wisdom, you should ask God, who gives generously to all without finding fault, and it will be given to you." (NIV)*

Remember when you encounter criticism, it's not over yet.

75 - Flex

Fred Astaire lived to be 88. He danced professionally until the age of 70, and he continued to be in excellent physical shape well into his 80s. He was 5 feet 9 inches tall and never weighed more than 136 pounds, which he believed to be his ideal dancing weight.

When asked the secret of his good health as he aged, he said he attributed much of his physical fitness to daily stretching.

Bob Hope lived to be 100, and he was also known for his vigor and robust health as he grew older. His career began in Vaudeville; he acted, sang, and danced his way to superstardom. At the peak of his career, he was the number one box office draw in the world. When asked the secret of his good health as he aged, he said he attributed much of his physical fitness to daily stretching.

George Burns capped a successful career as a radio comic with an equally successful career as a film actor. He was one of the most popular entertainers in America and lived to be 100. He was also known for his excellent health as he advanced in age. When asked the secret of his good health as he grew older, he said he attributed much of his physical fitness to daily stretching.

A study published in the 1990s said that women who had pursued a career in dance were as flexible and healthy in their 80s as women in their 30s. Researchers concluded that one of the key reasons for their good health as they aged was daily stretching.

Health researcher Dr. Robert Cooper writes, "You could look and feel several decades younger than your age by spending a few minutes a week sharpening some underrated skills-flexibility, agility, balance and coordination. How? By progressively developing your mind, senses and muscles in some new ways, with 5-minute stretches."

There seems to be an important lesson here: Learn to flex to start on the road to improvement. Find a stretching program that works for you and get started.

The Bible says to *"listen to advice and accept correction. Then in the end you will be wise."* (Proverbs 19:20 ICB)

76 - Yawn

Your cat sleeps an average of 15 hours a day and often sleeps 20 hours in a 24 hour period. Your dog sleeps an average of 13 hours a day but wakes up several times during sleep and is generally not as sound a sleeper as you or your cat. But how much sleep do you need?

The December, 2014 issue of the *AARP Magazine* deals with numerous health factors and says that new research indicates that eight to nine hours of sleep for humans is even more important than previously thought. The main article states that recent studies confirm that the brain "resets" itself during sleep and clears actual toxins from it's cells. These toxins are only cleansed during prolonged sleep of more than eight hours. One surprising research result found that a person has to sleep over eight hours to experience proper dream cycles. Studies of the brain function of Alzheimer's patients found that individuals with the disease no longer dream. One exciting element of the study is that a new brain chemical has been discovered that seems to actually induce dreaming and that chemical is produced by the brain during long periods of sleep. The chemical is thought to possibly be a protection against the development of Alzheimers.

Michael J. Breus. PhD and Stuart J. Meyers, M.D. give a list of some of the results of sleep deprivation.

1. When you reduce your sleep by as little as one and a half hours for even one night, your performance and alertness drop 32% the next day.
2. Less than eight hours of sleep impairs memory and interferes with cognitive function.
3. More moodiness is the result of lack of sleep.
4. Lack of sleep doubles your chance of an accident at work.
5. The National Highway Traffic Safety Administration says that

"drowsy driving" is responsible for 100,000 car crashes, 71,000 injuries and 1, 550 traffic deaths every year.

Maybe it's time to get a good night's sleep.

No wonder the Bible says in Psalm 127:2b, *"for he [God] grants sleep to those he loves." (NIV)*

77 - Be Careful What You Say

The following is a list of actual newspaper headlines.

Man Robs, Then Kills Himself

Mayor Says D.C. Is Safe Except For Murders

Boys Cause As Many Pregnancies As Girls

Prostitutes Appeal To Pope

Drunk Gets Nine Months In Violin Case

Dead Expected To Rise

"Dead" woman Doesn't Recall What happened

Hospitals Are Sued By 7 Foot Doctors

Two Convicts Evade Noose. Jury Hung

Lawmen From Mexico Barbeque Guests

Antique Stripper To Demonstrate Wares At Store

Today's Ballpoint is very simple. Be careful what you say and pay attention to how you say it. Communication is important in everything from business to marriage. Stop, take a moment and be sure you say what you mean to say.

The Bible says, *"He who guards his lips guards his life, but he who speaks rashly will come to ruin." (Proverbs, 13:3-4 NIV)*

Think before you speak. Be careful what you say.

78 - Do What It Takes

Bertie, the son of a saloon owner, grew up in the highlands of Scotland. He developed a fierce drive to succeed, so he worked at whatever would make money. He herded cattle as a child, shined shoes on local street corners, and worked as a day laborer, harvesting crops.

He had little education, so he taught himself shorthand at 13 years of age to enhance his chance for employment. He entered the University of Dundee as a teenager and studied his way to a degree. He worked as a newspaper reporter from 1897 to 1901. During that time, he decided to move to Johannesburg, South Africa, because he believed that city would provide greater opportunity. He did not make enough money as a reporter to afford the move, so he took an extra job cleaning toilets for two years. He was asked later in life if he felt humiliated at being a college graduate (when few people even attended college) and a working reporter who had to clean toilets. Bertie answered that, at first, he hated the menial job but knew it was necessary for him to reach his goal. He eventually learned to be thankful for the chance to clean toilets because it brought him closer to his dream.

Bertie made the move to South Africa, where he again became a reporter. He saved his money and again took any job available so he could immigrate to the United States. He arrived in New York City in 1904 and found a job at a local newspaper.

Bertie continued to work and save until his dream came true in 1917 when he founded his own business magazine. He decided to name it after himself. He used his last name and called it *Forbes Magazine*. The empire based on that magazine is now valued in the billions. It is a good thing B.C. Forbes was willing to clean toilets. They were the stepping stones to his success.

Are you willing to do whatever it takes to accomplish your goal? Forbes cleaned toilets without complaint because that brought him closer to the reality of his desires. What are you willing to do? Is your dream worth it?

The Bible says in Proverbs 13:19 that *"a longing fulfilled is sweet to the soul." (NIV)*

79 - The No-Complaint Zone

Sometimes a story is disturbing and difficult but contains a lesson so inspirational that it needs to be told. You are about to read that kind of story.

Christy Brown was born with congenital cerebral palsy resulting in total paralysis. He was born in 1932 at the height of the Great Depression. Christy was the son of an Irish bricklayer and one of 22 children. He was considered mentally deficient and given virtually no training or education. But when he was five years old, he picked up a piece of chalk with his foot and tried to write the letter A on the floor.

Christy's mother was so impressed by his effort that she taught him to read and write. A local doctor, Bob Collis, who happened to be an expert on cerebral palsy, volunteered to help the boy. Through a process of intense programs, Christy learned language and developed the ability to type with a single toe.

Christy Brown eventually married and became an author. His autobiography, *My Left Foot*, took 10 years to complete and was published in 1954. The book became a best seller and led to a published novel in 1970. The autobiography was made into an Oscar-winning film in 1987 with Daniel Day-Lewis as Christy. In his autobiography, Brown wrote, "My education was practically nil. The first and only bit of education I ever had was learning the alphabet from mother at the age of five. I had gone on from there the best way I could on my own, teaching myself to read books—mostly Dickens!—to learn all I could from them."

After Brown had established himself as an internationally known poet and artist, Dr. Collis, his original therapist, said of him that he was "proof of the amazing power … to overcome the impossible." The next time you are tempted to groan and complain about your difficulties, remember Christy Brown and declare your life a no-complaint zone. Get up, thank God for your opportunities, and get going. You can do what you need to do!

The Bible says in Philippians 4:13, *"I can do everything through Christ who strengthens me."* (GW)

80 - Read the Signals

Have you ever been stalked by a crow?

John M. Marzluff, a wildlife biologist at the University of Washington, conducted a fascinating study of crows and facial recognition. Marzluff marked seven crows with special tags then he put on a mask and attacked the crows. For the next two years, whenever he approached the crows wearing the same mask, the crows went crazy and dive-bombed the professor. If he removed the mask, the crows ignored him. Remember that this went on for two years. But the most remarkable finding was that the offspring of the crows would also attack the mask although they had never seen it (they had not hatched when the experiment began.)

Marzluff also discovered that crows have amazing powers of observation. They can memorize garbage pickup times over a several block radius and never be wrong. They can learn the exact sequence of traffic lights and use the signals to place nuts (they want cracked) under the wheels of cars. Again, they are never wrong.

If a crow can learn the right signals, then what do you think a human being can learn by carefully observing other people?

Let me give you an example: Scientists have discovered that how something feels has a dramatic effect. According to The De-Textbook: The Stuff You Didn't Know about the Stuff You Thought You Knew (edited by Jack O'Brien), men are more serious about decisions when they hold a heavy object. In one study, researchers found that men who lifted something heavy were much more likely to donate to a charity or be generous toward someone. Men who lifted a lighter object were less likely to give when asked. The researchers also observed that if a person (male or female) touched something with a rough surface, he would immediately see situations in a negative way. Surprisingly, the study also found that a person who sat in a hard chair during a negotiation was much more difficult to work with, whereas a person who sat in a soft chair was more conciliatory and easier to deal with.

These are signals that can alert you to what the other person is likely to do.

Learn to read the signals all around you. This is a skill that can improve your chance for success.

You are a complex and fascinating person. It is no surprise that the Bible says you are *"fearfully and wonderfully made [by God]." (Psalms 139:14 NIV)*

Can you think of a time when you misread a person? Would it have made a difference if you had had the skill to understand him better?

81 - Sleep Well

Henry Temple was elected to the British parliament when he was only 26. He came from an aristocratic family and was initially famous, not for politics, but for his fashionable style of dress.

For the next thirty years, Temple worked his way up through the ranks of the British system until he was appointed foreign secretary (equivalent to the secretary of state in the United States). His ambition was to become prime minister, but he seemed stuck in a cabinet position.

Everything changed for Temple when an incident erupted in Greece in 1850. A British citizen was illegally detained by the Greek government. When Temple confirmed the report, he flew into action. He shocked all of Europe when he mobilized the entire Royal Navy and sent it to Athens to free that single British citizen. The Royal Navy, under direct orders from Temple, confronted the Greek government. Because of the overwhelming military force against them, the Greeks capitulated and freed the British subject.

Controversy immediately exploded; Temple was threatened with the loss of his position. But the British public rose up and saved him. He quickly became the most popular leader in the land. When challenged to defend his decision, Temple refused to apologize and stated that he wanted the world to know that he would protect every British citizen, regardless of his location.

Years later, Temple, now 3rd Viscount Palmerston, finally became prime minister at 71 years of age (the oldest first-time prime minister in British history). Because of his natural brilliance and deep experience, the nation expected an exceptional administration, but Palmerston failed to deliver and lasted barely a year in office. What happened? The answer may shock you.

A.N. Wilson, one of the most respected historians in modern Britain, says that one personal factor ruined the leadership of this remarkable man: He didn't sleep enough. His friends and supporters noticed his growing fatigue and urged him to improve his sleep schedule. Even Queen Victoria warned him to rest more. Palmerston so wanted to fulfill his dream of being a great prime minister that he miscalculated his need for sleep and paid the price of inferior performance.

What about you? The National Sleep Foundation, after a two-year international study, confirmed that we need 8–9 hours of sleep EVERY night. The Foundation says that this is essential for what it calls "sleep health." The study mentions three things that help you sleep:

1. Limit caffeine (coffee, tea, soft drinks, and energy drinks) during the day, and no caffeine in the evening.
2. Try to deal with nothing agitating or upsetting after 8 p.m.
3. Go to bed at the same time every night.

Make sure you get enough sleep to power your life. This is important!

The Bible says, *"The Lord gives sleep to those he loves." (Psalms 127:2 ICB)*

82 - Mental Clarity

The following are things that have only happened once.

- In August 1964, the Beatles held the top spot on both the singles and albums charts in both the United States and the United Kingdom at the same time. Their single "A Hard Day's Night" was at No. 1 on the singles chart and the album "A Hard Day's Night" was No. 1 on the albums chart.

- An NFL team played against a CFL (Canadian Football League) team. On August 8, 1961 the Buffalo Bills lost to the Hamilton (Ontario) Tiger-Cats.

- A major disease was wiped out. In 1980, the World Health Organization announced that smallpox had been globally eliminated.

- The United States House of Representatives canceled itself. Although bad weather has closed the House several times, only once has it voted to close itself. It happened on October 24, 1877, so the members could attend a championship horse race at Pimlico Race Course.

- The United States government was completely debt free only once. For several months in 1835, during the administration of Andrew Jackson, all debts were paid and no money was owed.

New research indicates that your brain works better when you concentrate on only one thing at a time.

Dr. Daniel Levitin, professor of psychology and behavioral neuroscience at McGill University, quotes research that shows the human brain does not like multitasking. Dr. Levitin states that you begin to lose mental clarity and memory retrievability when you try to do two or more things at the same time. He thinks that mental overload is a big reason for an epidemic of routine forgetfulness, such as misplacing your car keys, forgetting where you parked, or losing the remote for your TV.

Dr. Levitin suggests that you can significantly improve your performance when you simply focus on one thing.

The Bible says in Proverbs 3:13, *"Blessed is the one who finds wisdom, and the one who gets understanding." (ESV)*

Use wisdom to improve your life.

83 - Move Up

Bernie Schwartz was a Jewish kid who grew up on the Upper East Side of New York City. When World War II intruded into American life he joined the United States Navy.

Bernie was well-liked by his fellow sailors and could always make his shipmates laugh. Once, while serving on a submarine escort in the Pacific, he tried a new approach to entertain the crew. He discovered that he had a talent for imitating characters in popular movies; he could even mimic their voices and acting styles. He was such a hit that he became a regular feature, filling in between the boredom and the kamikaze attacks.

When the war ended, Bernie used the new GI Bill to attend college, and he eventually landed in Hollywood. Because Bernie was unusually handsome, he was noticed by a representative of a Hollywood studio and offered a screen test. His striking looks and ease in front of the camera led to a part in a movie. The studio quickly realized that Schwartz had a powerful appeal to young women and decided to expand his opportunities.

Even with his looks and natural humor, Bernie had one big problem: He had difficulty shedding his heavy New York East Side accent. In one film, *The Black Shield of Falworth*, Bernie was given the line, "Yonder lies the castle of my father." But when he spoke it on screen, it sounded like, "Yonder lies duh castle of my fuddah." The girls still loved him.

Bernie, now renamed Tony Curtis, went on to one of the most successful movie careers in American film history. He even became known as "the writer's actor" because he developed such skill in delivering his lines. He obviously traveled far beyond his early limitations. He became such a good actor that it was said he could even give Robert De Niro lessons in how it was done.

The lesson here is that success can come to those who start but never stop. Bernie Schwartz started small and became big because he never stopped moving up. When he mastered one level, he immediately jumped to the next. He never stayed where he was. He always moved up.

Do you need to get unstuck? Have you been at your level too long? Is it time for you to move up? What are you waiting for?

The Bible says in Ecclesiastes 9:10, *"Whatever your hand finds to do, do it with all your might." (NIV)*

84 - Order

Jazz is considered by music historians to be the one musical form entirely invented in the United States. It's unexpected surges and surprising connections and switches continue to dazzle and entertain.

There are many famous jazz artists, some black and some white; but most agree the greatest was Louis Armstrong.

Armstrong was born in New Orleans in 1901 and died in New York City in 1971. His early life was a nightmare of disappointment and dysfunction. He was the grandson of slaves. When he was abandoned by both parents (he only saw his father when the man was marching in local parades), he was taken in by his grandmother. His neighborhood was so dangerous it was called "the battlefield."

Louie lived by delivering newspapers and selling discarded food back to restaurants. He was briefly enrolled in the Fisk School for Boys, where he was introduced to music, but he dropped out at age 11. His life was permanently changed when he was informally adopted by a Jewish family from Lithuania named Karnofsky. The Karnofskys gave the boy deep love and taught him self-discipline. That discipline carried over into his music.

When Louie was in his 20s, he migrated to Chicago, where he was "discovered" as a remarkable cornet and trumpet player. He was soon performing with some of the most famous bands of the era and rising to the height of his profession as the most famous and successful jazz musician in the nation.

Louie Armstrong was not only known for his virtuoso talent, he was also known for the stability and success of his life. While most jazz performers were crashing into a self-destructive cycle of drugs, alcohol, relationship malfunction, and financial mismanagement, Armstrong maintained a controlled and sensible life.

Respected poet and literary critic Clive James gives the secret of Louie's life when he writes, "Armstrong, with everything against him, knew how to lead an ordered life." He had learned well the lessons taught him by a generous Jewish family who simply decided to love him.

Dr. Daniel Levitin, in his book *The Organized Mind: Thinking Straight in the Age of Information Overload*, says that the one factor that sets apart the highly successful from the underachiever is the ability to order and organize life. There is power in an orderly life. Order is more than basic organization. Order is the ability to arrange your life to do what works best. It is the ability to allow "common sense" to keep you on the right path.

Orderly financial planning, orderly attention to your work, orderly commitment to your important relationships, and orderly development of your spiritual life can form a solid foundation on which to build your future.

What do you need to learn to live an orderly life? What do you need to know to progress forward? Get what you need and then get going.

The Bible says, *"But everything should be done in a fitting and orderly way." (1 Corinthians 14:40 NIV)*

85 - Embrace the Unexpected

James Basie was born in 1901 in Red Bank, New Jersey. His mother taught him to play the piano when he was a child. Basie soon showed significant musical ability and decided to pursue every musical opportunity in his hometown. When he was 16, he dropped out of school and got a job providing musical accompaniment for silent movies in the local theater. He eventually made it to Harlem, New York, where his talents helped him lead a band that he worked with for 50 years. When he died in 1984 in Florida, James (now known as Count Basie) was recognized as one of the most influential jazz musicians and big band conductors in American history.

All of this is common knowledge, but a little-known and unexpected incident changed his professional direction and secured his fame and success.

While performing on a national vaudeville circuit in the 1920s, Basie was unexpectedly stranded in Kansas City, Missouri. His tour fell apart, and he was stuck in what, at the time, was a rough, uncultured frontier town. Basie seemed to have landed in the middle of a disaster. But there was opportunity hiding in an experience that seemed negative on the surface. To Basie's surprise, the residents of Kansas City turned out to have a sophisticated and exceptional love for jazz. The city was already attracting hot, young, talented musicians.

Basie quickly realized that he had discovered an audience that could launch him to a higher level. He joined the leading jazz band in the city in 1929 and soon became its unchallenged leader. He and his band, now known as the Count Basie Orchestra, moved to New York City and became wildly popular. He became known as the "King of Swing" and changed the musical direction of the nation. Basie's greatest success was born in an unexpected detour of frustration and disappointment. His life was changed when he realized that his best opportunity was disguised as an unwanted interruption.

What about you? Are you alert to the possibilities all around you? Can you see opportunity in disappointment? Don't let your frustrations blind you to your future.

Make a list today of two elements of your life that seem negative. Examine them and write out every seed of potential success embedded in both situations. Make a new plan based on what you discover.

The Bible says, *"No one knows when his time will come."* *(Ecclesiastes 9:12 GW)*

86 - What You Have in Common With Slime Mold

Slime mold had its first starring role in the movies. The 1958 film *The Blob* (also titled *The Molten Meteor*) is an independent movie about an alien slime mold that arrives on a meteor that crashes in Downingtown, Pennsylvania. The Blob grows to a gigantic size, begins to digest every human available, and threatens the destruction of the town and, by extension, the whole earth.

Steve McQueen, in his first starring role at age 27, plays a teenager who battles the blubbering behemoth. The movie debuted as the second feature to *I Married a Monster from Outer Space* but soon surpassed the lead film in popularity, becoming a cult classic.

The Blob in the movie is actually based on real slime molds that have always coexisted with humans. These actual slime molds move in a similar way to the alien in the movie. Their movement is caused by a process called *chemotaxis*.

This process works when the slime mold senses the presence of a particular chemical (*chemo*) and moves toward it (*taxis*). The slime mold is attracted to appealing chemicals called *chemoattractants* and moves away from dangerous chemicals called *chemorepellents*. This means it is attracted to chemicals that can feed it and repelled by chemicals that can hurt it.

If you want to relate to how this works, imagine the difference between the delicious aroma of freshly baked chocolate chip cookies and the disgusting smell of skunk odor. You, then, have something in common with slime mold: You are attracted to something good and repelled by something bad. This also applies to your relationships. People are attracted to you when you are positive, happy, and encouraging. They are repelled when you are negative, critical, and complaining. Ronald Reagan understood this. Many historians say that Reagan was so positive and optimistic that even his enemies liked him. He accomplished more by being attractive.

Take a chance. Ask someone you trust if you tend to attract or repel. The answer may be critical for your future success or failure.

Even when (especially when) you deal with serious issues, make sure you do so in a compelling and persuasive way. All the other "slime molds" are waiting to respond.

The Bible says, *"Finally, brothers and sisters, whatever is true, whatever is noble, whatever is right, whatever is pure, whatever is lovely, whatever is admirable—if anything is excellent or praiseworthy—think about such things." (Philippians 4:8 NIV)*

87 - Out of the Box

The Battle of Diamond Rock was decided by an unusual tactic.

Diamond Rock is a basalt formation that rises 574 feet (175 meters) above the clear waters of the Caribbean Sea. It is the diamond shaped remains of a volcanic lava dome, located south of the town of Fort De France, on the island of Martinique.

British Admiral Samuel Hood quickly recognized its strategic value and hauled cannon and supplies to the summit in 1804. He placed 107 sailors on the rock and renamed it HMS Diamond Rock.

The British and French were embroiled in the Napoleonic Wars, so the French Navy decided to capture the rock and use it to harass British shipping. It was so easily defended that the British sailors resisted all attacks for 18 months. The French had no answer for the cannon that commanded the waters around the base.

They decided on one more assault and so attacked the British from May 31 to June 2, 1805, in what came to be known as the Battle of Diamond Rock. At first, the attacks were as useless as before; it seemed that the French would again fail. But then one of the French officers had an idea. Away from the view of the British sentries, the French filled a boat with barrels of rum. They included the boat in the next assault and deliberately allowed the boat to run aground at the base of the island. They then withdrew their warships in an apparent retreat, leaving the stranded boat.

When the defenders saw the departure of the French ships, they noticed the abandoned boat and sent a few sailors to investigate. The sailors found the rum and arranged to hoist the barrels to the top. The garrison drank the rum and became so intoxicated they were unable to withstand the next attack, just as the French had hoped. The rock fell to the French, and the hungover sailors were surrendered to British authorities.

An out-of-the-box idea won the battle and conquered the rock.

Do you need new ideas to conquer the "rocks" in your life? Is it possible that something that seems unlikely may be the key that unlocks your problem?

1. Take paper and write a brief description of an "unsolvable" situation.
2. Record as many possible approaches to a solution as you can think of in 10 minutes. Write everything that comes to your mind, even if it seems crazy.
3. Make a plan to try your ideas and see where they lead.
4. Continue until you find new ways to address your challenges. Find out what works.

The Bible says that *"people who cherish understanding will prosper." (Proverbs 19:8 NLT)*

Try to understand new ways to succeed.

88 - It's Never Too Late

Leroy Paige was born on July 7, 1906 in Mobile, Alabama. He may have been the greatest baseball pitcher of all time.

Leroy "Satchel" Paige played for years in the famous Negro leagues. In 1933, he won 33 games and lost only four, attracting the attention of the major leagues. Legendary New York Yankees player Joe DiMaggio said that Paige was "the best and fastest pitcher I've ever faced."

The most remarkable thing about Paige was his amazing longevity. He became the oldest major league rookie in history at age 42 and pitched in baseball's All-Star Game at age 47. He was 59 when he pitched three scoreless innings on September 25, 1965, for Kansas City. This made him the oldest active player ever to play the game. He played his last professional game at the age of 60. He was the first black baseball player to be inducted into the Baseball Hall of Fame.

Dr. Leila Denmark is another story of remarkable longevity. Dr. Denmark graduated from the Medical College of Georgia in 1928 and is recognized as the co-developer of the pertussis (whooping cough) vaccine. Dr. Denmark practiced medicine until the age of 103 and died at the age of 114, when she was officially acknowledged as the fourth oldest person in the world. Dr. Denmark was also my son Jonathan's pediatrician.

The last time we took Jonathan for a checkup, Dr. Denmark was 100 years old. She was bright, full of energy, and completely in charge of Jonathan's visit. She told us that to celebrate her 100th birthday, she went backpacking and tent camping in the Rockies of Colorado for two weeks, followed by three days of golf in Palm Springs, California. She felt great. When I asked about her diet, she said the only thing she insisted on was the consumption of a banana a day. (This is not medical advice, just a report of our conversation.)

The lives of Satchel Paige and Dr. Denmark demonstrate that it's never too late to live. They show that it is possible to be active and productive as life moves forward. If God still allows you to be here, then you are not finished. It's never too late to do something new. In fact, an attitude of adventure and exploration may even help you stay youthful.

Today, make a list of three things you have always wanted to try, three foods you have always wanted to eat, and three places you have always wanted to visit. Use your list to rev up your life. It's never too late to feel young.

The Bible says in Jeremiah 17:7–8, *"But blessed is the one who trusts in the LORD, whose confidence is in him. They will be like a tree planted by the water that sends out its roots by the stream. It does not fear when heat comes; its leaves are always green. It has no worries in a year of drought and never fails to bear fruit."(NIV)*

89 - The Ultimate Sacrifice

Martin August Treptow was a small town barber from the Midwestern United States.

Martin was born in Chippewa Falls, Wisconsin and grew up immersed in American values. He worked hard, went to church, loved his family and served his community. He was an active member of the National Guard and joined the U.S. Army in 1917 when his country entered World War I.

Martin was placed in the 108th Infantry of the 42nd Division and sent to France. On July 30, 1918 his army group was engaged in the Second Battle of the Marne where the allied forces eventually stopped the German offensive and saved Paris. His battalion was told to take Hill 212 of the La Croix Farm and as the fighting began an officer called for a volunteer to carry an urgent message to another battalion. Martin immediately offered to take the message and sprinted toward another section of the front. He was killed by artillery fire. Martin was 25.

After the attack, Martin's body was recovered and a diary was found in his pocket. In the diary were written these words, under the heading My Pledge, "America must win this war. Therefore I will work, I will save, I will sacrifice, I will endure, I will fight cheerfully and do my utmost, as if the issue of the whole struggle depended on me alone."

On January 20, 1981, Ronald Reagan was sworn in as president of the United States. In his inaugural address, he told the story of Martin Treptow and read his diary entry, which then became a part of the history of the occasion. Reagan finished with words that reminded all Americans that what was now required was "our best effort and our willingness to believe in ourselves and to believe in our capacity to perform great deeds, to believe that together with God's help we can and will resolve the problems which now confront us. And, after all, why shouldn't we believe that? We are Americans."

The unavoidable lesson from this is that some things are so important they are worth every sacrifice, even the ultimate one. America stands for personal freedom, commitment to morality, sanctity of the family, biblical principles, and individual opportunity unencumbered by a large and intrusive government. Martin Treptow gave his life for these ideals. What will you do?

The Bible says, *"Blessed is the nation whose God is the LORD."* (Psalms 33:12 NIV)

90 - Staying Young

The jellyfish species, *Turritopsis nutricula* looks like a creature from a science fiction movie. It is one of the strangest animals on earth.

This particular jellyfish is found in every ocean in the world. It is small, with an upper bell-shaped dome that is only half an inch wide. It is a certain shade of red and has around 80 tentacles that hang beneath the body. It floats elegantly through the water using its tentacles to capture food.

The most unusual thing about this jellyfish is that, unless it is injured or eaten, it never dies. When it reaches old age, it starts a process called transdifferentiation. In a manner completely unknown to science, the jellyfish signals its cells to change in a way similar to the cellular action of a salamander growing a new limb or eye. Every cell in its body transforms it into the tiny polyp it was at birth. It becomes an infant jellyfish again and starts the growth process toward adulthood and old age all over. This continues indefinitely, making the jellyfish biologically immortal. It simply becomes young again.

Advances in brain science have determined that you have the ability to rejuvenate your brain. You can help your brain become younger. Human performance expert Dr. Robert Cooper writes that, "whenever your brain cells are activated—by new sights, sounds, conversations, creative pursuits or problem-solving...—they instantaneously begin to change. They take in more electrochemical energy, form new connections, remodel nerve endings, improve receptor networks and revitalize brain function."

Michael Chafetz, PhD, a research neuropsychologist, adds that the key to age-proof living is "brain fitness—you must regularly challenge all aspects of your brain to expand its performance and slow or prevent its aging."

Let me suggest:

1. Try something new every day. Expand your experiences: Take a different route home; eat a new food.
2. Meet someone new each week. Grow your personal network and have fun.
3. Read an author or study a topic you are unfamiliar with. (Do this once a month.) Develop your intellect.

God made you to be the best you can be. Get growing!

The Bible says to *"praise the LORD ... who satisfies your desires with good things so that your youth is renewed like the eagle's." (Psalms 103:2, 5 NIV)*

91 - Prepare for the Unexpected

Eugene O'Neill was born in 1888 in a hotel room on Times Square in New York City, where a Starbucks now stands. His father was an Irish actor, so O'Neill spent most of his childhood living in hotels, boarding houses, and on trains. When he was 48, he won the Nobel Prize in Literature 1936.

In 1923, O'Neill finished a play he called *Strange Interlude*. It was not performed on Broadway until 1928 when it won the Pulitzer Prize for Drama. In one of its runs, the play was performed in Quincy, Massachusetts. Since the play was four hours long, O'Neill agreed to allow a dinner break partway through the production. He had noticed a restaurant across the street from the theater and decided to recommend that theatergoers use that restaurant exclusively so they could eat and still return to the show on time.

What O'Neill did not know was that the owner of the restaurant was desperate. He had built a pseudocolonial structure with a bright orange roof. He had put all his money into the venture and had produced attractive and exceptional food dishes. He had devoted long hours of work and commitment, but the business was on the edge of failure: He was $40,000 in debt (an enormous sum at the time) and on the verge of bankruptcy.

When the play opened, it was a smashing success. People came from several states, so the performances were sold out every night. Hundreds of patrons filled the theater, and those same hundreds flocked to the restaurant across the street. The diners liked the restaurant so much that when the play finally closed, they kept coming. They told their friends, and the restaurant became one of the most popular dining attractions in the region. Money poured in, and the restaurant became a beacon of success. The owner of the restaurant was so inspired by the turnaround that he decided to expand. He opened new facilities in several cities. The new restaurants were as popular as the first. Soon he began to build an empire.

By 1965, his restaurant chain was the largest in the United States and doing more business than McDonald's, Burger King, and Kentucky Fried Chicken combined. By 1970, the business had 1,000 restaurants and 500 motor lodges all over the country.

The desperate restaurant owner who was saved by Eugene O'Neill's play was Howard Johnson.

Here is the simple lesson: Always prepare for success. Always be ready for the unexpected; your answer may already be on the way.

Howard Johnson was ready when opportunity struck. He had already built his restaurant; he was prepared.

Are you working on your dream? Are you ready? Are you prepared for the unexpected?

Prepare for success. The Bible says that *"the plans of the diligent lead to profit." (Proverbs 21:5 NIV)*

92 - Loyalty

One of the oldest medieval documents tells the story of a knight that had been captured and imprisoned in a castle. The story says that two hundred of the knight's battle hounds, on their own, remembered their training, formed a battle line, attacked the castle and rescued their master.

Another ancient text tells the story of King Lysimachus of Persia. When the king died, his faithful dog threw himself onto the king's funeral pyre.

When the movie idol Rudolph Valentino died in 1926, his dog, Kabar, refused to leave Valentino's room. The canine stayed for two weeks, refusing all food and water, until he too died.

There is a well-documented account about a family from Indiana that went on a vacation in 1923. During the course of the trip, their dog, a collie, was lost. The family searched for the pet without success and finally decided to return home. Sometime after their return, they were contacted by a relative in Oregon who reported that the dog had traveled 2,000 miles to the farm in Oregon where it had been born. The dog was happily awaiting their arrival to pick him up.

When I was 11 years old, I was exploring a swamp near my grandmother's home. It was a frigid February day, and I was following a narrow path through a profusion of cattails. Suddenly the trail curved, and I stepped off into a side area. The surface was covered with ice. I broke through and fell into a deep, freezing pool. I called for help but didn't expect an answer because no one knew where I was. After a few minutes of thrashing in the water, my feet and legs began to feel numb. Then something unexpected happened: My dog, Checker, appeared. He stretched his neck toward me (he was a big dog, part huskie and part collie) and grabbed my arm in his mouth. He then walked backward until he had pulled me from the water. After a moment of recovery, I hugged my dog, and we headed home. I still wonder how he found me.

There is something special about loyalty. When you show loyalty, you demonstrate a deep commitment to another person. Loyalty is a cure for selfish motivation. When you are loyal to someone, you put him ahead of your needs and desires.

Let me suggest:

1. Be loyal to your wife or husband. No other vows are more sacred than the ones you spoke to one another at your wedding. Extend that loyalty to your children.
2. Be loyal to your friends. Give without expecting anything in return.
3. Use the loyalty test in all your relationships. My friend Mike Murdock says that you should only trust and work with people who honor you and are loyal to you.

The Bible says that *"love is patient, love is kind. Love does not envy, is not boastful, is not arrogant, is not rude, is not self-seeking, is not irritable, and does not keep a record of wrongs." (1 Corinthians 13:4–5 CSB)*

Be loyal.

93 - Act Young

The four main characters in the 1978 movie, *Grease* were all 18-year-old high school seniors. In reality, the four were played by actors much older. Danny was played by John Travolta, 23, Sandy was played by Olivia Newton-John, 29, Kenickie was played by Jeff Conway, 27, and Rizzo was played by Stockard Channing, 33.

The movies have always used older performers to portray younger characters. Some other examples are Harland Williams in the 2002 comedy, *Sorority Boys*. Williams played a character who was 21. He was 40. In the iconic film, *Ferris Bueller's Day Off*, Matthew Broderick was 24 when he played the lead role, a high school student.

Two of the biggest age gaps in movie casting history were in the films, *Joan of Arc* and the *Harry Potter* series. In *Joan of Arc*, Ingrid Bergman played 14-year old Joan when she was 39. In the *Harry Potter* films, Moaning Myrtle, who was the ghost of a girl killed at 14 (who stayed the same age as at her death) was portrayed by actress Shirley Henderson, who was 36.

One of the oddest casting choices was for the popular television show, *The Golden Girls*. In the series Estelle Getty, who was 62, played 86-year old Sophia. She was actually a year younger than Bea Arthur (63) who played her daughter.

In all of these examples, a much older actor was able to successfully impersonate someone decidedly younger. In every case the performer "seemed" younger by acting younger. They, of course, were helped by make-up, good lighting, and creative camera angles, but the core of their portrayals was the skill to act young.

I was recently at a welcome center in West Virginia. As I exited the restroom, I greeted two men who were also leaving. They both walked with poor posture, slumped, and weak. They spoke without energy and seemed old. When the men began to discuss their ages, I was surprised to discover that I was older than both of them. When I told them my age, they both said I had to be lying. I guess the rules of positive attitude and good health I have tried to follow must work.

The lesson is simple. People respond to what you project. If you project youthfulness and energy, people will perceive you as youthful and energetic; the more you project that image, the more youthful and energetic you will seem to yourself.

Stand up straight. Use good posture. Do everything with enthusiastic energy and see the response you get.

The Bible says in Isaiah 40:31, *"...but those who hope in the Lord will renew their strength. They will soar on wings like eagles; they will run and not grow weary, they will walk and not be faint."*

94 - Keep Going

There are an estimated 96 million rats living in New York City. That's 12 rats for every one person. The largest rat ever discovered was found living in a volcanic crater in New Guinea. It was identified as the Bosavi wooly rat, is the size of a housecat and weighs 4 pounds.

Rats are found in every environment in the world and have a number of unusual characteristics. They can learn through trial and error and rarely forget. An adult rat can jump 3 feet straight up from a standing position and can fall 50 feet without harm. It will not even be stunned, because rats have nearly perfect balance. A rat can swim continually for three days and squeeze through an opening the size of a quarter.

Rats have poor eyesight but have hearing far superior to a human, detecting sounds in the ultrasound range. Rats also have an extraordinary sense of smell. One rat can sniff the urine of another rat and immediately know the specific identity of the rat, it's gender and even it's stress level. They follow scent trails to food and to and from their lairs. Although rats usually live in filthy surroundings they are clean animals that lick and groom themselves daily.

Perhaps the most interesting rat fact is a rat's ability to chew through almost anything. If a rat has enough time it can gnaw through wood, concrete, steel and even glass, if there is the tiniest crack. In his book, *The Triumph of Seeds*, Thor Hanson writes that a rat in pursuit of a meal of seeds can chew through inches of solid steel and will keep chewing and chewing until it succeeds.

This is a valuable lesson from the common rat. The rat succeeds because it simply keeps going. There is power in persistence. You may be so close to your breakthrough that you cannot afford to quit. I heard a pastor recently refer to the biblical story of Joshua, a Jewish army, and the siege of the ancient fortified city of Jericho. He reminded us that God told the Jews to march seven times around the city, stop to blow trumpets, shout, and then the giant city walls would collapse. But what would have happened if they had stopped at six times around the wall? They would have failed. Sometimes you just have to keep marching.

Don't give up. You may be on your sixth march and not know it. One more march and your obstacles will fall. Be like the rat: Keep chewing until you break through.

The Bible says, *"When the trumpets sounded, the army shouted, and at the sound of the trumpet, when the men gave a loud shout, the wall collapsed; so everyone charged straight in, and they took the city." (Joshua 6:20 NIV)*

95 - Unique

What do world renowned pianist Arthur Rubinstein, Italian dictator Benito Mussolini, famous Indian mathematician Ramannujan, Nobel Prizewinning economist Gary Becker and physicists Albert Einstein and Edward Teller (father of the atom bomb) have in common? They are all geniuses and they were all children who started talking much later than other children in their age group.

Edward Teller did not speak until he was 4 years old. Einstein did not speak until he was 3, but he was not fluent with words until age 9. Although most late talkers are boys, Clara Schumann (famous 19th-century pianist) and Julia Robinson (first woman elected president of the American Mathematical Society) were also verbally delayed.

Members of Mensa (a society for people with high IQs) are known to have more allergies than the general population, and students enrolled in the prestigious Johns Hopkins University special program for children with exceptionally gifted mathematical abilities show unusual characteristics unrelated to math. Four out of every five students have allergies and/or nearsightedness and/or left-handedness.

Thomas Sowell, in his book *The Einstein Syndrome: Bright Children Who Talk Late*, writes that "there are a number of disabilities that are more common among people of high intellect than in the general population." Sowell further writes that "no one really knows for sure why this is so."

Always remember that you are unique. There has never been or ever will be anyone like you. Everything about you makes you who you are. Your abilities and disabilities, your strengths and weaknesses, all combine to produce you. There is something exceptional about you that may be hidden by an apparent disadvantage. Einstein did not speak for years, but his mind was exceptional. Most of the students in the Johns Hopkins program struggle with a limitation but have exceptional mathematical abilities. God has planted something special and important in you; you just have to find it.

Let me suggest:

1. Take a notebook and list advantages that come from your weaknesses. Find at least three.
2. List everything (no matter how small) that you are good at.
3. Develop what you discovered in the first two exercises.

The Bible says in Psalm 139:14, *"I will praise You [God] because I have been remarkably and wonderfully made." (HCSB)*

96 - Celebrate Yourself

Elvis Presley gave his first musical performance on October 3, 1945 at the Mississippi-Alabama State Fair and Dairy Show. The 10 year old stood on a chair and sang the Red Foley song, "Old Shep." He came in fifth in the competition.

Nine years later, Elvis traveled to Memphis, Tennessee, to visit Sun Records. The receptionist Marion Keisker remembers Elvis asking if he could pay to make a demo recording as a gift for his mother. The shy nineteen-year-old then added that he was also curious to hear what his voice sounded like (biographer Peter Guralnick thinks Elvis secretly hoped he would be "discovered").

After a few moments of introductory conversation, Keisker asked Elvis what kind of singer he was, and Presley replied, "I sing all kinds." Not satisfied, the receptionist pushed harder and asked Presley to describe his musical style. She recalled the young man answering, "I don't sound like nobody."

Elvis paid the fee, made the demo, and the rest, as the saying goes, is history.

What made a teenager from rural Mississippi with no musical training and no stage experience think he had a future as a singer? What inspired him to travel to Memphis, risk ridicule and rejection, to spend the little money he had on a demo that he had no guarantee anyone would even hear?

I think there is a clue in something Marion Keisker remembered. When challenged to describe his style, the young Elvis simply said, "I don't sound like nobody." He believed in his gift; he celebrated his dream.

I have a friend who always tells people to "never let anyone steal your dream." History is packed with stories of people who fearlessly and relentlessly pursued their personal visions. Elvis was right; he didn't sound like nobody and neither do you.

God made you. You are not an accident of mindless evolution. You are alive for a reason. You are special. Celebrate yourself, and don't let anyone steal your dream.

The Bible says, *"So God created man in his own image, in the image of God he created him; male and female he created them."* (Genesis 1:27 ESV)

97 - Resilience

Frederick Winter of Michigan recently became the oldest competitor to complete the 100-meter dash at the National Senior Games. He finished the race in 42.38 seconds. Winter is 100 years old.

Winter did two tours of duty for the US Navy in the Second World War and continued to stay fit after his military service. Winter says he eats right (he likes salmon) and does 30 minutes of aerobics at 6 a.m. every morning.

Dan Pellman in 2015 became the first 100-year-old to run the 100-meter dash in 27 seconds. He completed his race in San Diego, California, on a day when the temperature reached almost 100 degrees.

When I was in college, I was notified that my great-grandmother had been hospitalized and was dying. I was urged to come home as quickly as possible. (I would often visit my great-grandmother on her working farm on the Left Fork of Bull Creek in eastern Kentucky. I enjoyed the visits because she was intelligent, feisty, outspoken, and deeply Christian. She had an infectious love of life and a vigorous positive attitude. She overflowed with fun and high spirits.)

When I received the message about her impending death, I left school and headed for home, hoping to arrive before her passing. At that time, my great-grandmother Lafferty (she was my mother's grandmother) was in her early 90s and still worked her farm by herself.

When I arrived at the hospital, I hurried in and asked for my great-grandmother's room number. I was told that there was no number available because "she was gone." My heart fell, and I asked when she had died. The nurse looked puzzled and said, "She's not dead; she's gone."

I located my mother and father and asked what had happened. This is the story I was told: When my great-grandmother woke up in her room (after being transported by ambulance and connected to numerous monitors and IVs), she sat up, glanced around, and said, "I've had enough of this." She then removed all the needles, got out of bed, dressed, and exited. The nurse was left helplessly protesting. My great-grandmother walked 3½ miles home and never went back. She collapsed and died peacefully a few years later while working in her garden.

These three people have (or had) something in common: They all have (or had) resilience. They all are (or were) tough, and that toughness helps (or helped) keep them active and full of life and energy. Harvard Medical School published a study several years ago that listed resilience (mental toughness) as a dominant factor in long life and good health. Resilience is a mental refusal to worry. It is a determined attitude of belief, a conviction that "I can handle this."

Resilience in your thoughts, resilience in your attitude, and resilience in your approach can fortify you for a healthy and fruitful life. For me, resilience is grounded in my trust in a loving heavenly Father who will always care for me. That is my rock of resilience.

Whatever you do, be tough; be resilient.

The Bible says, *"The righteous will flourish like a palm tree, they will grow like a cedar of Lebanon; planted in the house of the LORD, they will flourish in the courts of our God. They will still bear fruit in old age, they will stay fresh and green."* (Psalms 92:12–4 NIV)

98 - The Happiness Genius

I passed through a hyper-serious phase in my twenties. I loved parties and people but became convinced that I needed to clamp down my gleeful tendencies and increase my capacity for serious living. Everything worked well at first, but soon I moved into a pattern that did not allow any relaxation or casual enjoyment. I was on a path to emotional suppression when I encountered the Happiness Genius.

This happiness genius surprised me with insights and guidance that released me from a grim approach and redirected me to the sunnier side of life. This person rescued me and taught me that happiness is an energy we all need. I eventually fell in love with the happiness genius (her name is Amy) and married her.

My wife follows a few simple rules. One major rule is to focus on what makes you happy and draw strength from the experience. This does not mean that she believes a person should do morally wrong things just because they temporarily make a person feel good. That would be shallow and dangerous. But she does believe that finding and enjoying what makes you happy is a major source of power and energy.

Let me tell you some of the ways Amy experiences happiness. (The specifics may be different for you, but the principle is the same.) Amy decorates for every season and every holiday. This week our house looks like a fall festival with pumpkins, mums, and scented candles everywhere. People bring their children to see our scenic front porch. Soon the house will change to Thanksgiving and Christmas (by far, Amy's favorite time of year). At the beginning of the new year, Amy will transform our home into a winter wonderland. She does all this because "it makes her happy." It makes our family and friends happy as well. Amy prefers to watch movies and read books with happy endings. Why? Because they make her happy. She loves to discuss positive plans and ideas that can make other people happy. Why? Because she deeply cares about people and wants to make them happy. Whenever she discovers friends or neighbors who are sick or troubled, she puts together gift boxes to take to them. She is hoping to make them happy.

Amy recently read *The Life-Changing Magic of Tidying Up: The Japanese Art of Decluttering and Organizing* by Marie Kondo. When I asked her what she liked best about the book, she said she especially liked the author's advice on decluttering a closet. Kondo writes that you should hold each piece of clothing and ask, "Does this give me joy?" Amy likes that concept because it uses happiness as a measure of good decision-making. This does not mean that joy or happiness are the only factors in a good decision but simply a reminder of their importance.

Last night, Amy sat on our living room couch, drank a cup of hot tea, and watched a Christmas movie (it's October). Why? Because it made her happy. She does not agonize over what to do with her free time. She just picks what makes her happy; it's very uncomplicated.

It is no surprise that Amy gave our daughter, Allison, the middle name Joy. It represents how she wants to live life. I am thankful God led me to Amy. Living with a happiness genius has immeasurably enriched and blessed my life. I think Amy may be on to something special. Why don't you look at your life and decide to find and enjoy all the happiness you can? Then you can use the energy from all that happiness to increase the happiness of people around you. You too can be a happiness genius.

The Bible says in Proverbs 17:22, *"A cheerful heart is good medicine."* (NIV)

99 - Make Your Fears Flee

Beware the Beast of Bladenboro.

One day in 1954 in the small town of Bladenboro, North Carolina, an animal was found with its skull crushed and all the blood drained from its body. The men who found the carcass were puzzled that no part of the animal had been eaten. Soon other slaughtered animals were found, including dogs, goats, and small livestock. All had their jaws broken, their skulls crushed, their blood completely drained; and none had been eaten. The local people began to panic.

Eventually, several residents claimed to have seen the beast responsible for the attacks. It was described (by all the different eyewitnesses) as dark in color, around 150 pounds. It emitted a weird sound (they said) similar to the loud wail of a baby or the hysterical cries of a high-pitched woman's voice.

Professional trackers were hired and reported finding strange marks made by large cat-like paws. The creature also seemed to drag a long tail, which left a trail that resembled the movement of a giant snake. Bloodhounds were given the scent found in the tracks but, curiously, all of them refused to follow the trail, regardless of the urging of their owners.

It was at this point that the residents of Bladenboro decided to fight back. Members of the community began to carry guns everywhere they went. People refused to give in to their fears, and they determined to restore their regular routines. The town raised money to hire several professional big game hunters, and plans were made to hunt and kill the beast.

So many hunters responded that soon the town overflowed with tough, vigilant, armed men. Patrols were organized and sent to search the rural areas around the community. Then suddenly, the attacks stopped. The beast was never seen again. To this day, its identity is a mystery; it never returned.

The residents of Bladenboro gave the smartest possible response to fear: They fought back. Everything changed when they decided to face their fears and attack the source of their threat. When they confronted their fear with action, their fear (and the beast) disappeared.

This is your best strategy to make your fears flee. Stand up and face your fears; often they will vanish like smoke. Even if they prove real, you will still be better off because your action can lead to solutions. A plan to defeat fear is always better than a retreat into denial and avoidance. You can only deal with what you are willing to face.

The Bible says in Psalms 34:4, *"I sought the LORD, and he answered me; he delivered me from all my fears." (NIV)*

100 - An Early Start

When our daughter Allison was 8 years old, a financial mentor advised us to remove her allowance ($5.00 per week) and teach her to make money.

When we stopped the allowance, Allison's response was immediate: negative and intense. She vigorously proclaimed our mistake at every available opportunity (especially to her grandparents). She debated us (she was very good) until she realized that Amy and I were determined.

Allison then turned her considerable willpower to addressing her financial situation. She sold cookies (limited success); she wrote, composed, and sold a neighborhood newspaper (more successful because she thought to include positive articles about each of the neighbors). She consistently worked hard and was thrilled when she made more than her allowance after her first allowance-free month.

Her breakthrough came when she had an idea. Because she was in elementary school, she used pencils. She realized that other kids not only used but also exhausted their pencils, and they would always need to buy more. Her great insight combined that realization with another idea. She had been deeply influenced by the positive attitudes she encountered as she helped us with my career as a Christian motivational speaker and trainer. She believed that if children her age could be exposed to positive encouragement, they could more easily move up a solid success track. She decided to create school-ready pencils imprinted with positive slogans. Her first design read, "ATTITUDE IS EVERYTHING," followed by "YOU CAN DO IT" and "BELIEVE IN YOURSELF AND YOU WILL SUCCEED."

For more than a dozen years, she promoted her business

(soon named Positive Pencils International). She monitored her success, expanded at every opportunity, and tithed her profits to her church and other Christian causes (especially the children's radio programs of Focus on the Family).

Her entrepreneurial spirit led her to apply to Law School after graduating from college. She was accepted, finished, and later admitted to the Kentucky Bar. She clerked for a judge for a year, served as an assistant county attorney prosecuting child abuse cases for four years, and eventually became a bankruptcy attorney.

She then felt called to run for state office and used her proven entrepreneurial skills to run a state-wide campaign. After winning the Republican primary, she was decisively elected state treasurer of Kentucky (the state's chief financial officer) by 22 points. Her 571,000 votes were the highest vote total for any candidate of either party (including governor).

You cannot predict the consequences of early choices. God used Allison's early training and positive response to the option we gave her to help her develop the attitude and discipline of success. You cannot overestimate the importance of starting early and starting right. You are sowing the seeds of your future today.

The Bible says, *"For whatever a person sows he will also reap."* (Galatians 6:7 CSB)

101 - BIG

The baobab tree, native to Africa, is one of the biggest tree species in the world. The trunk grows up to 30 feet thick and many local tribal groups use the trees for accommodations. Once a tree is selected, it is hollowed out and various rooms are created for families to inhabit. The tree is known for its unusual shape, with giant limbs extending upward that more resemble roots than limbs. Because of it's odd appearance an old Arab legend states that the trees were mysteriously uprooted and replanted upside down.

In December 1970, a specialty hotel was opened on one of the slopes of mighty Mount Everest. The hotel, which sits at 12,800 feet above sea level, is reached by taking a flight from Katmandu or hiking 12 days to the resort location. The beds are designed with oxygen tanks, and all rooms have stunning views of 15 of the highest mountains in the world.

In the late 19th century, architect James Lafferty (my mother's maiden name is Lafferty, but I know of no connection) designed a strange building in Margate City, New Jersey. It was shaped like an elephant that was using its trunk to drink from a water trough. The design was huge: 60 feet long, 65 feet high, and topped by an observation deck made to look like a howdah (the traditional platform used to ride elephants in India) overlooking the Atlantic Ocean.

In 1883, Lafferty designed an even larger elephant structure on Coney Island, New York. It was 122 feet tall and housed a cigar store in one front leg, an elevator in another, and stairways in each of the hind legs. People could rent rooms in whatever part of the elephant they preferred. It burned down in 1896.

All of these unusual structures had one thing in common:

They were all BIG.

When I was starting my speaking career, a friend recommended that I read a book written by a Georgia State University professor. I bought the book but did not read it for several months; I thought the title was interesting but simplistic. When I actually read the book, I was blown away. That short book altered the way I looked at life and success. The title, *The Magic of Thinking Big*, expressed the powerful idea of the book. I am different today because I chose to believe its contents.

How big do you dream? How high do you reach? How far do you want to go? One thing is certain: You will only achieve to the level of your biggest goal.

1. Take a moment to pray for God's guidance.
2. Write on a piece of paper an outrageous, insane, happy goal that you can only get with God's help.
3. Record what you are willing to do to achieve that goal.
4. Get started!

The Bible says in Ephesians 3:20 that God *"is able to do immeasurably more than all we ask or imagine, according to his power that is at work within us." (NIV)*

WOW!! That's BIG.

102 - It's Not About You

Many of you are not aware that C.E. Crouse recently retired. The reason you are not aware of this is that most of you don't know C.E. Crouse.

C.E. Crouse worked a number of years as a founding partner of a public accounting firm in Indianapolis, Indiana. He has been faithfully married to Lolita for several decades and is close to his children and multiple grandchildren. He is 6 feet 8 inches tall, enjoys large SUVs (he needs them), and small towns. He always wears cowboy boots, which add even more to his considerable height.

C.E. grew up in a small town in Kentucky where his father was a wealthy and successful business owner. His relatives include the Luce family of Fort Valley, Georgia, who built the Blue Bird Body Company (known for their school buses) into one of the largest and most respected companies in that industry.

Last week, I attended a tribute dinner to honor C.E. and his wife. People came from throughout the United States to recognize the achievements of this remarkable man. The governor of Kentucky and the mayor of the community where the dinner was hosted both provided special awards.

The reason for all of this acknowledgment was that C.E. had not only retired from his corporate firm, he had also retired from serving (for 23 years) as the chairman of the Board of Trustees of Asbury University, a highly regarded 126-year-old Christian institution. During his tenure, he invested thousands of hours, traveled thousands of miles, served with exceptional dedication, and guided the university through the terms of seven presidents. He was the stable core of a significant organization. He did all of this with a sunny approach and intelligent leadership. He fought battles, but because of his fair and honest administration, he never made an enemy. One more thing, he never received financial compensation for those years of service and sacrifice; he served for free.

I have served on the board of trustees with C.E. for the past eight years. His example has inspired my life. The reason so many people arrived last Friday to give tribute to this man is because they recognized the greatness that is based on contributing to the lives of other people.

The lesson from this personal "Ballpoint" is simple: Greatness is not about you; it is about what you do for other people. If you want to be unhappy then choose selfishness. If you prefer happiness, choose to give. Service is God's path to greatness.

People surged forward to honor this man because of what he had done for them and their children. People will come forward to honor you when you spend your life honoring and helping them.

The Bible says that *"God loves a cheerful giver." (2 Corinthians 9:7 NIV)*

103 - How to Win

It was a blazing hot day. When the temperature reached 101 degrees people began to visibly weaken. Small children cried and complained continually as the relentless heat baked everyone.

Because the asphalt had only been laid that morning, the sidewalk and street surfaces began to melt; a number of walkers had the shoes sucked off their feet, leaving them stranded in the melting mess.

A small group of selected guests had been invited, but an additional 28,000 people stormed in using counterfeit tickets. The huge number of extra visitors overwhelmed restaurants and other facilities. Food and drink were quickly exhausted, and people could not find refreshment.

Because of a plumber's strike, the owners had to choose between working toilets and water fountains. They chose the toilets (good idea), which left the crowds without drinking water (and in such heat).

A gas leak closed the main attraction and forced the surging mobs into fewer areas, which only increased the overcrowding.

A giant, meticulously detailed replica of a famous boat took on so many passengers that it came close to sinking; people had to be hastily escorted off.

The local and national news media mocked the day as "Black Sunday" and predicted total failure for the project.

It was July 17, 1955, and Disneyland had just opened.

When the crowds had gone and the doors locked, Walt

Disney made a decision. He called together his executive team and announced that the day had given them a tremendous opportunity. The experience of handling 28,000 unexpected people moving around in an unfinished park had given them the chance to learn how to run such an operation in reality and not in theory.

Disney then organized and guided a special task force, which studied every detail of the disaster and developed the plans that eventually led to the superbly run and fabulously successful parks of today.

Very simply, Walt Disney knew how to win. He knew how to learn from difficulties, how to regroup and move forward. Do you?

This is a year of untapped possibilities and unseen potential. It is inspiring to imagine what you can do with this year if you have this kind of Disney attitude.

With this positive approach, you can believe the best, expect the most, and press forward. You can find a way to win.

The Bible says in Proverbs 24:3, *"By wisdom a house is built, and through understanding it is established." (NIV)*

104 - Strike Quick

The fastest recorded knockout in a professional boxing match happened in Lewiston, Maine on September 29, 1946.

Fighter Ralph Walton was in his corner waiting for the opening bell when he decided to adjust his protective rubber mouthpiece. He had just inserted his fingers into his mouth when the bell rang. Walton looked up to see his opponent, Al Couture, running toward him. Before Walton could remove his fingers, Couture quickly punched him in the face and knocked him to the mat; Walton was unconscious. The fight was over; it had lasted half a second.

Lewiston, Maine, was also the site of the heavyweight championship fight in 1965 between Sonny Liston and Cassius Clay (later known as Muhammad Ali). Most fans were still finding their seats when Clay suddenly knocked out Liston in the first round with a (still debated) "mystery punch." The fight had only started 1 minute and 57 seconds earlier. The bout lasted five more rounds, but Liston never fully recovered from the first-round knockout. Clay won and became the undisputed heavyweight champion of the world in one of the most dramatic matches ever. Sports Illustrated voted the fight the fourth greatest moment in sports history.

The news media captured Clay, in one of the most famous scenes in modern sports, yelling to the crowd, "I am the greatest!"

In both these stories, the advantage went to the man who struck first. Both winning fighters seized an immediate opportunity and rammed themselves into their future. They did not hesitate; they moved fast.

How many significant opportunities are lost because of the

failure to act quickly? When you know what you want and are satisfied that the goal is worthy, then the best choice may be to move fast.

For years, I have taught a principle I call QRT, which stands for Quick Response Time. I learned the importance of this the hard way. I lost a major financial opportunity by waiting for the perfect moment to move. The perfect moment never came, and the deal died. I already had researched my options and invested a substantial amount; I knew the best course, but my delay cost me. It took a long time to recover from the losses of that lost opportunity. I was not quick enough.

When you have examined your situation and are satisfied that you have found the best path, strike quickly. It may be your only chance to win.

1. Do your diligent research.
2. Make up your mind.
3. Strike.

The Bible says that "the plans of the diligent lead to profit." (Proverbs 21:5 NIV)